"Good books on preaching are many. Great ones are few. I regard this one among the great, because it advances novel proposals and covers ground generally overlooked. The authors are well qualified by training, gifting, and longtime practice. They have a burden for congregations not just to know but to love the Bible. They know the key to a congregation that is strong in the word is pastoral preaching that opens up the whole of Scripture, not just cherished bits and themes. Most importantly, they have a plan—calmly articulated but revolutionary in its way—and wise, strategic suggestions to move church leaders toward a more effective grasp and disclosure of *the entire* Bible's deep nourishment and challenge. They lay out this plan with skill, tact, and compelling insight."

**Robert W. Yarbrough,** Professor of New Testament, Covenant Theological Seminary

"Tim Patrick and Andrew Reid have served the church well in this book. Their aim is to encourage and aid pastors in preaching through the whole Bible cover to cover, and to do so in a way that is informed by biblical theology, systematic theology, and the gospel itself. The book is thoughtful and practical, with many helpful diagrams and lists. The authors are rightly concerned about biblical illiteracy in churches. As they point out, even in churches where the Bible is expounded, it can be done in ways that don't help the person in the pew gain a grasp of the whole counsel of God. This work is a very useful addition to the literature on preaching and one that ably addresses that need."

**Graham A. Cole,** Dean, Vice President of Education, and Professor of Biblical and Systematic Theology, Trinity Evangelical Divinity School; author, *He Who Gives Life* and *Faithful Theology*

"Practical 'how-to' advice from the school of experience is always welcome, and there is a wealth of it here, challenging the expositor to focus and think through issues that are rarely, if ever, considered. How should our preaching schedules faithfully reflect the *whole* counsel of God, as well as the pastor's heart for the long-term welfare and nurture of the congregation? It will be a stimulating challenge and tonic for the more experienced preacher, but will prove especially valuable to those in the earlier years of pastoral ministry."

**David Jackman,** Former President, The Proclamation Trust

T0339332

"As individuals, we are positively influenced by our favorite Bible passages. We return to them to form our lives, and we use them to teach and encourage others. Of course, we are negatively influenced by the Bible passages we do not know, do not read, and do not use. This limits our growth and maturity, and also limits our usefulness to others. In the same way, churches are positively influenced by their favorite Bible passages and negatively influenced by the Bible passages they do not know! While our evangelical theology may be that the whole Bible is the word of God, our evangelical culture may lead us to neglect most of it. Here is a robust challenge to preachers to ensure that we preach every part of the Bible—a big call for preachers and for churches! How good to be reminded to look for the maximum God has revealed rather than the minimum we can get away with!"

**Peter Adam**, Vicar Emeritus, St. Jude's Carlton; Former Principal, Ridley College, Melbourne

"Patrick and Reid have done a great service to working pastors. After considering theological foundations for preaching through the whole Bible, they give very practical instructions and tools for how to do it. Here are the answers to questions many younger preachers are asking about how to organize and maximize the impact of their work in the pulpit."

**Darrell Young**, Associate Director of International Workshops, Asia, Charles Simeon Trust

"So many Christians have simply lost the plot—that is, if they ever knew there was a plot. They have never been shown how the Bible as a whole tells the true story of the universe, from creation to new creation, governed by the sovereign mission and purpose of God, with the gospel of the Lord Jesus Christ as its integrating center. The result is a crippling ignorance of what it means to live consistently as participants in that great drama of Scripture, instructed by the Bible's historical revelation, and in expectation of God's mission accomplished. This book's rich theological reasoning and practical suggestions will motivate pastors to rectify that deficit by taking even more seriously their calling not just to preach ad hoc from the Bible, but to preach from the whole of the Bible over time, in such a way that their people grow in understanding the whole plan of God across the full canon of Scripture and live purposefully and fruitfully in the light of it (Col. 1:9–11)."

**Christopher J. H. Wright**, International Ministries Director, Langham Partnership; author, *The Mission of God: Unlocking the Bible's Grand Narrative*

# The Whole Counsel
of God

# The Whole Counsel of God

## Why and How to Preach the Entire Bible

Tim Patrick and
Andrew Reid

WHEATON, ILLINOIS

*The Whole Counsel of God: Why and How to Preach the Entire Bible*
Copyright © 2020 by Timothy R. C. Patrick and Andrew Reid
Published by Crossway
    1300 Crescent Street
    Wheaton, Illinois 60187

Cover design: Spencer Fuller, Faceout Studios

Cover image: Shutterstock

First printing, 2020

Printed in the United States of America

Unless otherwise indicated, Scripture quotations are from the ESV® Bible (The Holy Bible, English Standard Version®), copyright © 2001 by Crossway, a publishing ministry of Good News Publishers. Used by permission. All rights reserved.

Scripture references marked NRSV are from *The New Revised Standard Version.* Copyright © 1989 by the Division of Christian Education of the National Council of the Churches of Christ in the U.S.A. Published by Thomas Nelson, Inc. Used by permission of the National Council of the Churches of Christ in the U.S.A.

All emphases in Scripture quotations have been added by the authors.

Trade paperback ISBN: 978-1-4335-6007-1
ePub ISBN: 978-1-4335-6010-1
PDF ISBN: 978-1-4335-6008-8
Mobipocket ISBN: 978-1-4335-6009-5

**Library of Congress Cataloging-in-Publication Data**
Names: Patrick, Tim, 1974– author.
Title: The whole counsel of God: why and how to preach the entire Bible / Tim Patrick and Andrew Reid.
Description: Wheaton: Crossway, 2020. | Includes bibliographical references and index.
Identifiers: LCCN 2019014548| ISBN 9781433560071 (tp) | ISBN 9781433560095 (mobi) ISBN
   9781433560101 (epub)
Subjects: LCSH: Bible—Homiletical use. | Preaching.
Classification: LCC BS534.5 .P38 2020 | DDC 220.072—dc23
LC record available at https://lccn.loc.gov/2019014548

Crossway is a publishing ministry of Good News Publishers.

| V P | 28 | 27 | 26 | 25 | 24 | 23 | 22 | 21 | 20 |
|-----|----|----|----|----|----|----|----|----|----|
| 14 | 13 | 12 | 11 | 10 | 9 | 8 | 7 | 6 | 5 | 4 | 3 | 2 | 1 |

To Robert Miller,
who apprenticed me in preaching
through the books of the Bible
in the local church.

—Tim Patrick

To Denesh Divyanathan and Andrew Cheah,
friends and gospel partners,
who have graciously invited me to share with them
in the privilege of training young Asian pastor-teachers.

—Andrew Reid

# Contents

# Illustrations

# Foreword

I was delighted when I heard that my friends Tim Patrick and Andrew Reid had started on this book, and doubly delighted when I read the finished product. I'm confident that their work will be immensely useful for pastors and those training pastors in the great work of preaching the whole counsel of God.

Over the past twenty years or so, a large proportion of the conversations I've had with fellow preachers (and latterly with students) have revolved around the very issues that are dealt with carefully and graciously in this book. The challenges of how to preach the larger books, how to ensure a "balanced diet" of Scripture, how to ensure that our preaching is both rigorously textual and deeply theological, as well as how to balance exegesis, biblical theology, and systematic theology are enduring questions for every generation. In addition, ongoing questions around topical versus expository preaching are perennial causes of debate. This book most helpfully tackles such deeply practical questions in a principled and richly theological way.

You probably will not, of course, agree with everything you find in these pages. That's the nature of any book that seeks to be of genuine practical help to the preacher working in the local church context. The more finely grained the argument becomes, the more we encounter minor differences of approach. But I suspect the enduring value of this book will be not in persuading everyone of how many chapters of Isaiah to preach at a time, but rather in encouraging and fostering a thoughtful, realistic, theologically rounded, and literarily sensitive approach to preaching the whole of Scripture in the local church. That is a priceless contribution to make to the work of the gospel, and one that has been significantly neglected in recent times.

This book is also extremely timely. After the resurgence of expository preaching in the English-speaking world over the past fifty years, I suspect we are in danger of starting to assume its advantages rather than celebrating and promoting them. As is always the danger with a movement reaching its second and third generations, there is a growing tendency to drift away from a confidence in God doing his work through his word. Even amongst like-minded "word people," it is very easy to slip into an unconscious pragmatism that sees the key to health and change lying in other approaches. This book provides a sane and compelling rationale for God-honoring, word-centered ministry, which is vital for the progress of the gospel and the flourishing of the church of the Lord Jesus Christ.

Gary Millar
Queensland Theological College
Brisbane
March 2019

# Preface

This book was motivated by our love for the Lord and his church. In writing it, we were driven by our twin convictions that the church is established and grown by the word of the Lord, and that the Lord is rightly honored when the church sits under his word. While none of this would seem to be in any way controversial among evangelical Christians, the sobering reality is that a great deal of the Bible—perhaps, in fact, the majority—is never preached to the people of God, even in evangelical churches. There may be many reasons for this, and we will explore some of them in the chapters that follow. But whatever they are, we are worried that the practice of preaching only *parts* of the Scriptures necessarily results in the church being underfed and the Lord being only partly honored. In this volume, we want to address those problems by putting forward the case that vocational preachers should work to preach the *entire Bible* to their congregations and by offering some suggestions for how it might be done. In its essence, the concept is not complicated, but there is much to say about it given that so many of today's preaching programs are a long, long way from the ideal.

Part 1 has three chapters that tease out the importance of preaching the whole Bible, the many different ways that preachers fail to do that, and some of the troubling implications of offering less than the entirety of God's word to his people. This is followed by the central challenge of the book, which we might have called our "audacious" or "outrageous" challenge, except that we think it is neither of those things. Rather, we believe that a practical commitment to preaching through the whole Bible is completely consistent with the teaching found within the Bible itself, as well as with our doctrines of Scripture and the canon. Next, Part 2 offers five chapters that serve as something of a "how-to" guide, first showing the importance of theological frameworks for preaching across the whole Bible, and second offering some nuts-and-bolts advice for planning balanced long-range preaching programs. Finally, Part 3 has four chapters in which we consider the ways that our challenge fits in with the real-world issues that face any preacher who leads a busy and complex ministry.

We have been excited to work on this book as a joint project, recognizing the richness that comes from bringing two minds and two sets of pastoral experience to the conversation. Sharp readers may discern our unique voices at different points in what follows, but we trust that they too will see the benefit of our collaboration.

Tim is deeply grateful to the Bible College of South Australia for its most generous research and writing provisions, and for the wonderful colleagues who all share a passion for bringing the whole Scriptures to the people of God. He is also thankful to the various congregations of St. Jude's Anglican Church in Melbourne—especially Unichurch and those of the Parkville campus—for their time spent together learning through whole books of the Bible. On the home front, he cannot say enough about the constant support received from his wife, Catriona, who is as precious a partner in ministry as she is in all of life. Andrew would like to thank the board of the Evangelical Theological College of Asia for giving him the time to write in his early and critical days as principal, and also the congregations of St. Matthews Church in Shenton Park, the church plant of Curtin Community Church (both in Perth), and Holy Trinity Doncaster in Melbourne. Each of these churches loved the word of God and their pastor expounding it each week, and it was a delight to minister among them. However, before them was always Andrew's most prayerful and sharpest critic—his wife, Heather—who often found herself awakened early to hear the final product after having already talked the passage through while walking the dogs numerous times in the preceding week. Both Tim and Andrew must thank Justin Taylor and the Crossway team for their most professional and caring support throughout the entire writing and editing process. We are also both indebted to Kim Folland, Tim's executive assistant, for her excellent work in text editing and document formatting. Any faults that remain in the text are entirely our own.

# Introduction

One of the most disturbing stories in the Old Testament tells of Jephthah, one of the judges of Israel (Judg. 11:1–12:7). Jephthah is not known for his marvelous victory over the Ammonites. Nor is he known for his rise from obscurity and destitution to be the head of the tribe of Gilead or a judge of Israel. No, he is known for a terrible vow he made. It ended in him presenting his only daughter as a burnt offering (11:29–40). If you read Jephthah's story in the context of the Old Testament narrative, you find what lay at the roots of his deed. Although he appears to have been zealous for the Lord, Jephthah simply did not know the Scriptures. He was theologically deficient and lacked knowledge of what God had revealed in his word. This can be seen in his negotiations with the king of Ammon in Judges 11, as well as in his vow and failure to back out of it as it appears that God allowed him to do.

The point is that the people of God need to know God and his ways, but they cannot know God and his ways without knowing his word. This raises a critical question: How can God's people know the fullness of God's word unless it is constantly held up before them and systematically explained to them? In many places throughout the Bible, we see that this kind of commitment to the Scriptures—the entirety of the Scriptures—is indeed meant to characterize the people of God and to shape their activities. For example, Deuteronomy 17:18–19 gives a key requirement for every future king of Israel:

And when he sits on the throne of his kingdom, he shall write for himself in a book a copy of this law, approved by the Levitical priests. And it shall be with him, and he shall read in it all the days of his life, that he may learn to fear the LORD his God by keeping all the words of this law and these statutes, and doing them.

Similarly, as part of Joshua's commissioning to succeed Moses, Deuteronomy 31:9–13 speaks of the place of the word of God in the annual pattern of Israel's life:

Then Moses wrote this law and gave it to the priests, the sons of Levi, who carried the ark of the covenant of the LORD, and to all the elders of Israel. And Moses commanded them, "At the end of every seven years, at the set time in the year of release, at the Feast of Booths, when all Israel comes to appear before the LORD your God at the place that he will choose, you shall read this law before all Israel in their hearing. Assemble the people, men, women, and little ones, and the sojourner within your towns, that they may hear and learn to fear the LORD your God, and be careful to do all the words of this law, and that their children, who have not known it, may hear and learn to fear the LORD your God, as long as you live in the land that you are going over the Jordan to possess."

Chapter 8 of the book of Joshua records the people of Israel coming together for a covenant renewal ceremony. Verses 34–35 say,

Afterward he read all the words of the law, the blessing and the curse, according to all that is written in the Book of the Law. There was not a word of all that Moses commanded that Joshua did not read before all the assembly of Israel, and the women, and the little ones, and the sojourners who lived among them.

Generations later, the kingdom of Israel became divided and suffered many years of decline into sin and faithlessness, which was due to their abandonment of the word of God. But in the reign of the young King Josiah, the Book of the Law was rediscovered in the temple, and there followed a time of some renewal. Second Kings 23:1–3 tells how Josiah began his reforms:

> Then the king sent, and all the elders of Judah and Jerusalem were gathered to him. And the king went up to the house of the LORD, and with him all the men of Judah and all the inhabitants of Jerusalem and the priests and the prophets, all the people, both small and great. And he read in their hearing all the words of the Book of the Covenant that had been found in the house of the LORD. And the king stood by the pillar and made a covenant before the LORD, to walk after the LORD and to keep his commandments and his testimonies and his statutes with all his heart and all his soul, to perform the words of this covenant that were written in this book. And all the people joined in the covenant.

Moving forward many more years in the history of Israel, to the time of the restoration after the exile, we find Ezra again bringing the entirety of the word of God to the people of God as the nation is being reestablished. The event is found in Nehemiah 8:1–8 and is worth quoting at length:

> And all the people gathered as one man into the square before the Water Gate. And they told Ezra the scribe to bring the Book of the Law of Moses that the LORD had commanded Israel. So Ezra the priest brought the Law before the assembly, both men and women and all who could understand what they heard, on the first day of the seventh month. And he read from it facing the square before the Water Gate from early morning until midday, in the presence of the men and the women and those who could understand. And the ears of all the people were attentive to the Book of the Law. And Ezra the

scribe stood on a wooden platform that they had made for the purpose. And beside him stood Mattithiah, Shema, Anaiah, Uriah, Hilkiah, and Maaseiah on his right hand, and Pedaiah, Mishael, Malchijah, Hashum, Hashbaddanah, Zechariah, and Meshullam on his left hand. And Ezra opened the book in the sight of all the people, for he was above all the people, and as he opened it all the people stood. And Ezra blessed the LORD, the great God, and all the people answered, "Amen, Amen," lifting up their hands. And they bowed their heads and worshiped the LORD with their faces to the ground. Also Jeshua, Bani, Sherebiah, Jamin, Akkub, Shabbethai, Hodiah, Maaseiah, Kelita, Azariah, Jozabad, Hanan, Pelaiah, the Levites, helped the people to understand the Law, while the people remained in their places. They read from the book, from the Law of God, clearly, and they gave the sense, so that the people understood the reading.

The core conviction of this book is that the need for God's people to hear the whole Scriptures read and explained continues today. A light, thin, hotchpotch diet of Scripture—even well-taught Scripture—is not what God wants for his people, and yet this is all that too many churches offer. This book is written to help pastors and teachers of God's word make the fullness of that word known to their people over a lifetime of preaching. Our hope is that through such comprehensive preaching, God's saints might be better equipped for their roles than Jephthah was—that is, that they might know the mind and purposes of God, and so be equipped for every good work (2 Tim. 3:17).

We have set ourselves two specific tasks in writing. First, we wish to encourage preachers to make it their goal to preach the *entire* Bible because we are convinced that *all of it* is the word of God for us. This is a much bigger aim than simply saying that we want to encourage preaching *from across* the Bible. We are not just saying that we want to encourage the feeding of Christian congregations with a good sampling of many parts of the Scriptures. Rather, we want to promote the preaching of the whole Bible! We are conscious that whole-Bible preaching is such a monumental ambition that some might feel immediately that it is impossible even to contemplate it, and we are quite prepared to accept that for a range of very understandable and practical reasons, many, if not most, preachers will never be able to achieve complete success. However, our second purpose in writing is to present a number of paradigms and very practical helps that should allow most preachers to have a really decent shot at preaching through the entire Bible over long-term ministries to their congregations. As we lay out these suggestions, we are also convinced that even if preachers never quite end up bringing every single part of the Bible to their congregations but maintain it as their working goal to do so, they will at least end up offering a far fuller, more balanced, and even-handed program of teaching than they would by taking any other approach. There is nothing to be lost in aiming high.

Given these two purposes, it should be clear that this is not at all a book about *how to preach* a sermon. There are already many excellent books giving instruction on preaching, ranging from those that introduce the rookie to the basics of pulpit work right through to those that can stretch and deepen the most seasoned preacher.[1] Instead, this book is about *what to preach*, and about *how to plan and manage a long-range, ordered, and deliberate preaching program.*

---

1. Some volumes we would recommend include Peter Adam, *Speaking God's Words: A Practical Theology of Preaching* (Leicester, UK: Inter-Varsity, 1996); Murray Capill, *The Heart Is the Target: Preaching Practical Application from Every Text* (Phillipsburg, NJ: P&R, 2014); Allan Chapple, *Preaching: A Guidebook for Beginners* (London: The Latimer Trust, 2013); Dale Ralph Davis, *The Word Became Fresh: How to Preach from Old Testament Narrative Texts* (Fearn, Ross-shire, Scotland: Christian Focus, 2006); Sidney Greidanus, *The Modern Preacher and the Ancient Text: Interpreting and Preaching Biblical Literature* (Grand Rapids, MI, and Leicester, UK: Eerdmans and Inter-Varsity, 1988); Timothy Keller, *Preaching: Communicating Faith in an Age of Scepticism* (London: Hodder & Stoughton, 2014); Eugene L. Lowry, *The Homiletical Plot: The Sermon as Narrative Art Form*, exp. ed. (Louisville: Westminster John Knox, 2001); Haddon W. Robinson, *Biblical Preaching: The Development and Delivery of Expository Messages* (Grand Rapids, MI: Baker , 1980); John R. W. Stott, *I Believe in Preaching* (London: Hodder & Stoughton, 1982).

## Why a Book Like This Is Needed

In light of the standard evangelical convictions about the nature of Scripture, it would seem that it ought to be very commonplace for pastors and teachers to work toward preaching through the whole Bible for the people they serve. And yet the reality is that it is not. This is not only sad, but also somewhat ironic, given the heritage of the church in the Western world since the Protestant Reformation.

In the medieval period, despite the fact that the Mediterranean region was highly controlled by the Roman Catholic Church, the Bible was not very accessible. Even if people could afford their own copy (which would have been incredibly expensive before the days of the printing press), most would not have been able to read it. This was partly due to low literacy rates, but also because the main authorized version of the Bible was in Latin—the language of high scholarship—and not in the languages of the European peoples.

It was against this backdrop that the Protestant Reformers translated, mass-produced, and widely distributed the Scriptures. Their work cut directly across the priorities of Rome and so was incredibly dangerous. Indeed, some who pioneered the translation and promulgation of the Bible in English, such as William Tyndale and John Rogers, ended up paying with their lives. But they were willing to prioritize this task because they recognized that there was no greater need than for people to have access to the word of God.

Today, we Protestants have inherited not only the convictions of the Reformers, but also the reward of their great sacrifice, with churches and individual Christians around the developed world—and beyond—now having easy access to the Bible. In fact, *billions* of copies of the Bible have been printed, and it is by far the best-selling and most widely distributed book in history. The whole Bible has now been translated into well over five hundred languages, and more translations are being worked on all the time. If we think only about English speakers, we are humbled to find that we have too many Bible translations to even be able to keep track of them all; there have been hundreds! With growing literacy rates, cheap printing and transport costs, and increasing access through technology, more people than ever before can now read the Bible for themselves. In terms of access to the word of God, the Western world has come a long, long way since medieval times.

However, despite our common convictions about the Bible and the virtually unrestricted access to the Bible that was won at such cost, large numbers of people today are not at all familiar with the breadth of the Bible's teaching. What is particularly worrying about this is that it is true not only of non-Christian people, but too often, and increasingly, of Christ-professing, church-going, Bible-believing Christians. The idea seems to be a contradiction: Bible-believing Christians not knowing their Bibles. But it is too often the reality. It may be true that many faithful believers today have a favorite Bible verse or two, and some may even have memorized a good number of verses. Many may know lots of the famous Bible stories, perhaps in more detail than is often given in Sunday school classes. Some may even have reading patterns that take them through the whole of the Bible regularly, and many no doubt have a truly deep and sincere love for Jesus as Lord and trust in him as their Savior. But if you were to ask them, for example, how the Old Testament book of Joel fits into the grand story of the Israelite people, they would not know. If you asked what is the turning point of Mark's Gospel, they would again be stumped. If you asked what 2 John teaches, they would have no idea at all. In fact, it might even be possible that if you asked them to look up 2 John in their Bibles, some might have no idea where to turn and might instead end up in John 2.

Now, to be clear, none of this implies that the quality or "realness" of people's faith is a function of their Bible knowledge or that Bible scholars are the best and most praiseworthy Christians. Any such suggestions could quickly lead into all kinds of very wrong and dangerous thinking, to say nothing of their being completely against the core truths of the gospel itself. However, such trivial examples do again highlight the most significant question: How can it be that sincerely committed Bible-believing Christians who now have mostly unhindered access to the Scriptures—and whose spiritual forebears saw no greater priority than providing that access to the Scriptures—can still have relatively thin biblical knowledge? It is clear that Christian engagement with the Bible is not singularly proportional to access.

Of course, a simple explanation as to why many believers do not know their Bibles as well as they might is simply that they are not reading them enough. Profiting from our Reformation heritage, it may be that we own several copies of the whole Bible in our first language, but it may also be that we have left many of their pages unturned. Undoubtedly, in our honest moments, a good number of us would confess that our laziness and distraction are major factors contributing to our lack of Bible reading, and therefore our lack of Bible knowledge and consequent personal Christian formation. Indeed, when we hear the preacher at church conclude his sermon with the oft-repeated application point that we need to be reading our Bibles more, we rightly feel convicted.[2] We probably *should* be reading our Bibles more.

But while it would be wrong to completely ignore such matters of personal responsibility and discipline, in this book we actually want to turn the tables a little to ask some questions of those who are set apart as preachers, pastors, and teachers of the word. Could it be that many believers' limited Bible knowledge is a product of the limited biblical teaching they have received Sunday by Sunday in their churches? Could it partly be the case that some of them do not dedicate regular time to reading right through the Bible

---

2. Throughout this book, we refer to preachers using masculine pronouns on the general understanding that lead teachers of local churches—who are the primary audience of this work—will be male. However, we also recognize and hope that much of what we say is valuable for others, too—trainee or associate pastors, elders charged with appointing teaching pastors, congregation members taking responsibility for their own diet of Scripture, and women teaching women (e.g., Titus 2:3–4).

because they do not see their pastors preaching right through the Bible in their weekly sermons? Could it be that some do not feel equipped to engage with every part of the Bible because they have only ever heard a limited selection of Bible passages expounded for them by their pastors? Perhaps their piecemeal reading and studying of Scripture is just a reflection of what they have seen modeled by their ministers of the word. Even if they are regularly told to read their Bibles, what are they seeing modeled and what is being done for them week by week in church?

The reality is that few church members rise above their leaders. What Christians see pastors do is often what they do themselves. What they see them failing to do, they do not consider to be important. So if a pastor does not teach from the Bible, his sheep are unlikely to pick up their Bibles. If a pastor pulls a single verse out of the Bible without any reference to its context, it should not be surprising if the people he oversees similarly use the Bible like some kind of spiritual lucky dip. If a pastor has a few favorite passages or themes that he seems to return to over and over again, the members of the congregation may well also narrow down their Bible reading to those few "central" texts that seem to communicate all that God wants us to know and that do duty for every part of the Christian life. In all of these cases, the pastor is teaching the people that they do not really need to engage with the whole Bible in order to live and grow as disciples of Jesus.

When things are put as starkly as this, many Christians immediately and instinctively recoil. Few of us would consciously devalue the Bible in this way. However, what we believe in principle is not always what we adopt in practice, and this is true when it comes to teaching and learning the Bible. In order to find out how extensively our beliefs really shape our practice, perhaps it would be a revealing exercise to investigate when your church last heard an expository sermon from, say, the book of Jeremiah. If it has been a very long time, or it has never happened, might that indicate that for some reason your church does not think that God has anything particularly important or relevant to say through his words inscripturated in that biblical book? Taking it a step further, perhaps if your church records did tell us that there had been a sermon on Jeremiah in recent times, it could still be quite sobering to see how long it has been since you last had a whole sermon *series* on Jeremiah. And then—lest you feel overly confident about how your church's preaching program is standing up to this kind of scrutiny—would it even be worth looking to see whether you had ever had a sermon series that systematically preached *through the entire book* of Jeremiah, chapter and verse? In writing this book, we surveyed the preaching records of one well-known preacher with a lengthy pastoral ministry that was mostly connected to one church, and we found that his preaching on the historical books of the Old Testament was restricted to sixteen sermons, four of which were on Ruth. Another Bible-teaching church had recorded many great biblical sermons, but the ministers had preached from only nine Old Testament books in a nine-year period, and mostly in series that did not work through the whole book.

Of course, we can ask these kinds of questions with more than just the big Old Testament books on view. It is unfortunately true that many local churches have not even heard the entirety of one of the four Gospels preached through in a methodical way in living memory, but have instead heard only a range of sermons from different Gospel passages at different times. Perhaps some were delivered in six- or ten-week-long sequential preaching series, but when added together, even these did not cover the whole book. Undoubtedly there could well have been many faithful and quite excellent sermons delivered in these series. However, we are now asking not just whether there has been any serious exposition of individual passages of Scripture, but rather whether there have been any attempts to exposit the books of the Bible as they were written and intended to be read: as coherent wholes that together with other books of the Bible form a corpus that is recognized as the fullness of God's deliberate and enduring revelation.

The reason for pressing this point—including inflicting the sting of this kind of examination into our patterns of preaching—is because it helps us recognize a few very important things. First, it demonstrates that while we who preach may hold to a high view of Scripture theoretically, in practice we have perhaps only ever aspired to feed our flocks on limited parts of it rather than on everything that God has spoken to his world. Second, it might make us realize that we have not been as deliberate and long-range as we should have been in our planning of what we will preach to the church. Finally, it could also make us wonder whether we may have unintentionally communicated some things about the Bible that we do not really want to say: that some parts of it are not so important, and that the way God has ordered it is not particularly meaningful or useful for us. None of these thoughts are welcome for pastors or preachers, and we do not raise them here only with the intention that preachers turn to lamenting their failures, but rather as a stimulus for thinking frankly about preaching programs and how they can be made stronger.

We do hope and pray that you will come on this journey with us and benefit from it. We believe that it is quite possible to plan to feed the flock on a full diet of Scripture and to make good progress in achieving that end. We also believe that teaching according to such a long-range program will be used by God to deepen our people's grasp of Scripture, and their understanding of who he is and of his full plans and purposes. Ultimately, we trust that this book will result in God's people being better equipped to live well as his servants in his world for his glory, and will help them to avoid some of the unwanted outcomes of having just a shallow and piecemeal knowledge of Scripture.

PART 1

# THE IMPORTANCE OF PREACHING THE WHOLE BIBLE

1

# What the Bible Says about the Bible (and about Preaching)

Famines affect masses of people. Many die, with children often being the first. During the writing of this book, one famine continued to drastically unfold in Yemen. Famines are terrible and terrifying events wherever and whenever they occur. Their terror stems from the fact that they strike the very core of human existence: our need for sustenance—food and water—to maintain our health. It is perhaps for this reason that God uses the analogy of a famine at various times in the Bible. The most striking is Amos 8:11–13, where God declares the most disastrous famine for the people of God: a famine of hearing his word.

In this chapter, we seek to lay the groundwork for ensuring that the people for whom preachers have responsibility before God do not suffer such a terrifying spiritual plight. We want to start by getting our thinking right about what the word of God is and does, and then to focus on two particular passages of Scripture that are addressed to leaders of congregations and that give advice as to how they should think about the task of proclaiming the word of God to the people of God. We will also give some consideration to what the Bible says (or does not say) about preaching as the means of communicating the word of God.

## The God Who Speaks

The first page of Scripture tells us much about God. However, undoubtedly one of the most striking things that we see and hear is that he is a God who speaks, and whose speaking has its desired effect.[1] Repeatedly we hear, "And God said, 'Let there be . . .' And it was so" (Gen. 1:6–7, 14–15). This pattern continues as the story of Scripture is told. It is dominated by God speaking to his people and by God's words doing what they are intended to do. The life of Abraham was crafted by God speaking to him, calling him, and making promises to him (Gen. 12:1–3; 15:1; 17:1–22). Similarly, those descended physically and spiritually from Abraham were people of a God who speaks. Moses heard God speaking from the flaming bush, and this encounter set the course for his ministry and for the deliverance of the Israelite people from Egypt (Ex. 3:4–22). Moses also went up Mount Sinai to hear God speak all of his covenant laws that would govern his relationship with his people throughout Old Testament times (Exodus 19–31). The prophet Samuel heard God speaking out loud to foretell judgment on those who had rejected him and to appoint the first kings of Israel (1 Sam. 3:1–14; 9:15–17; 16:1–12). The main condemnation of King Saul was that he did not listen to or obey the right sounds (1 Sam. 15:6, 13–16, 19, 22–24, 26). Elijah, who represented God against the evil King Ahab and the prophets of Baal, repeatedly took his direction from the words that he heard God speak (e.g., 1 Kings 17:1–9; 18:1; 19:9–18). The Psalms record the love that the people of God had for his words (e.g., Psalms 1; 19; 119). The later prophets heard and sometimes formulaically repeated the words of God for the people (e.g., Jer. 2:1–3:5; Obad. 1–21; Hag. 1:1–7; Zech. 1:3–6).

---

1. For a fuller theology of the word of God spoken and written, see Peter Adam, *Speaking God's Words: A Practical Theology of Preaching* (Leicester, UK: Inter-Varsity, 1996).

And Jesus himself is presented to us in the opening lines of John's Gospel as the Word of God incarnate (John 1:1–18). We could go on and on, but the simple point is that in Scripture, our God presents himself from beginning to end as a speaking God.

That it is "in Scripture" that we find God to be a speaking God is very significant, as Scripture itself is the word of God not just spoken out but also written down. The Bible consists of words from God that are relevant and important to all people in all places at all times. The Bible does not directly engage all of the fine details of everyone's life and times, but it preserves and communicates the words of God that address the most important and constant aspects of the human condition, and it gives the explanations and guidance needed by all people for good and right living.

Written words should not be thought of as being more stale or less personal than audible spoken words. Indeed, the written word is powerful in ways that the spoken word is not. From a purely human perspective, one reason for this is that we tend to be far more deliberate, thoughtful, and structured with our written words. Although in the age of social media people do tend to write without thinking, more frequently it is spoken words that deliver unfiltered stream-of-consciousness communications. Written words, on the other hand, are usually more carefully considered, more helpfully structured, and more crisply expressed. Consider examples as broad as anniversary cards, legal contracts, memorial plaques, scientific reports, and corporate strategic plans. In all of these cases, the written words carry a sense of significance, permanence, and accuracy that is greater than the same words would have if they were only spoken. Of course, there can be very powerful spoken words, but even most great speeches are carefully drafted and prepared, so that these spoken words are actually a reading of written words, with all the benefits they bring. Further, the texts of many speeches are often distributed in written form after they have been delivered so that the words that were spoken can be experienced over and over again by many people.

God does not need to write his words down to ensure they are well-considered, well-structured, and well-presented, but he has given us some of his words in written form so that they might be permanently preserved, accurately copied, and then broadly distributed to, and received by, many people who can read them over and over. The Bible is God's means of communicating to all people the fixed things he wants all to hear.

It is worth pausing to reflect for a moment on what it would be like if God had not providentially and graciously enabled us to have his enduring and universal words in the Bible. How would we know him, ourselves, our true needs, or our purpose otherwise? We would have to rely on individual senses of what we feel God's will to be at any point. If we did not trust our individual internal senses, we might turn to nature to see what it might be able to teach us of God. Now, while the Bible does indeed say that nature can tell us some things about him, it also says that this is only a small part of what we really need to know, and we certainly could not deduce the gospel from our own observations or reflections; it is a nonintuitive message that needs to be passed on verbally (Rom. 1:19–20; cf. 10:14–15; 1 Cor. 15:1). We might instead take an anthropological approach and decide that we can learn about God from looking at all the world's cultures and religions to find some common points that we could assume were universal truths. Or we might resign ourselves to the fact that God, if he exists, is largely silent and ultimately unknowable. But the good news is that while we might not completely dismiss all of these other means of learning about God, he has given us the Bible, his unchanging word that we need for our well-being and that all the people of his world need to hear for their well-being. All we have to do is read it, hear it, and, for preachers, preach it to others too.

## What the Word of God Does

As we read God's words in Scripture, we come to know God as he wants us to know him, and our understanding of him is shaped by what he has communicated, not what we have imagined or specu-lated. Importantly, the Bible also sets the limits of our understand-ing and forces us to humbly accept that where it is silent, we must remain trustingly ignorant and confident that, in his goodness, God has not deprived us of any knowledge that we need in order to be true and faithful to him (2 Pet. 1:3–4).

But the Bible does more than just give us information. It is more than a big book of facts for us to learn. The words of God in the Bible do a great many other things. For example, they capture abstract notions, describe details, direct actions, affect relation-ships, explain events, explore ideas, express emotions, inform situ-ations, permit freedoms, promise hope, recount history, request participation, warn of danger, and more. It is very important for preachers to understand all of the different things that the words in the Bible do, because if they do not, their preaching can easily end up like a dry and old-fashioned form of lecturing in which the only goal is to transmit information. But through all that they do, the words in the Bible are meant to *shape us*. They are meant to determine not only what we believe, but also how we conduct every facet of our lives. The application of sermons must be more than the standard triplet of "Read your Bible," "Pray," and "Tell people about Jesus," because while all of these things are great biblical priorities, they do not exhaust all that the Bible says to us, or all that it does in and for us.[2]

One reason that evangelical preachers have sometimes been slow to suggest that the Bible does more than only inform us about faith in Jesus is that over the past half-century or so, there has been a great concern to protect the doctrine of justification by faith. Protestant Christians rightly recognize that this is one of the non-negotiable, central concepts in the Bible and that the greatest threat to its clean transmission is any idea that Christians

---

2. See Murray Capill, *The Heart Is the Target: Preaching Practical Application from Every Text* (Phillipsburg, NJ: P&R, 2014) for an excellent approach to application of bibli-cal texts in preaching.

gain salvific benefit from the things they do. By God's grace, our justification comes by our faith in Jesus as the Savior who paid the price for our sin so that we can stand before God himself. Nothing we do can either add to or subtract from the work of Jesus. The worst of sinners and the most morally upright of people stand in the same relationship to God. We are either justified by our faith or we are not justified at all. The things we do, either good or bad, are not part of the equation. Other than the fact that this is the plain teaching of the New Testament, the reason for wanting to defend this doctrine so vigorously is easy to understand. If we admit any form of justification by works, we immediately relativize or diminish the sacrifice of Jesus. It becomes something that is not technically necessary, and we therefore lose our comprehension of our real spiritual need, of God's grace toward us, of the thankfulness we owe him, and of the unquestionable centrality of Jesus in the purposes of God. In short, our whole theological framework begins to collapse.

As plain as it is that we must not distort the doctrine of justification by faith, sometimes our zeal for it can lead us to pit this belief against the Bible's call for obedience and good works. If we go too far, we can end up essentially saying that our morality is no longer important, and even that seeking to do and be good is bad because that might undercut our belief that it is exclusively through Jesus that we have God's saving acceptance. Of course, if we do get to this place, we have made the mistake of letting a doctrine drive our understanding of the Bible rather than letting the Bible determine our doctrinal convictions, because as much as the Bible holds up justification by faith, it never does that at the expense of obedience and disciplined living. The relationship between our faith and good works is, in fact, spelled out quite clearly in a number of places in the New Testament (e.g., Eph. 2:8–10; James 2:14–26). We are to be people of faith as we receive the free gift that transforms us from children of darkness into children of light. But that transformation also makes us want to be completely obedient to the words of God.

All of this is important to preaching because it means that the work of preachers is not done when they have preached Romans 1–5 to their congregations and established the doctrine of justification by faith. As they continue to preach through to the end of Romans, and then through the rest of the Bible too, they will need to give voice to so much more of what God is saying to his people and his world. Like the Bible, their preaching should be life-shaping as well as faith-shaping, and the integration of faith and life should also become clearer as more of the word of God is proclaimed. However, this will not happen if preachers do not have some practical commitment to the whole of Scripture, and lesser preaching risks the growth and perseverance of the people of God who are under their care.

Having laid some of these larger foundational points, it will be helpful for us to turn to two key passages in the New Testament where the apostle Paul explains to Christian leaders the importance and the shape of a word-based ministry.

## The Whole Counsel of God (Acts 20)

The first passage comes in the midst of Paul's defense of his ministry and final teary exhortation to the Ephesian elders in Acts 20:17–38. He is on his way to Jerusalem bearing a collection that he has been taking up among the churches that he had founded and ministered in. In his haste to arrive by Pentecost, he can spare only minimal time. So he sends for the elders, and they come to him in Miletus, where he addresses them in what is his only recorded address in Acts to a Christian audience. It ends with a deeply affectionate and sorrowful farewell, with tears on both sides indicating their shared deep love for one another. However, the content of the address gives us a wonderful glimpse into the motivations behind Paul's ministry and the way those motivations were fleshed out in practical ways when he was among the Ephesians.

Toward the end of his speech (Acts 20:27), Paul tells the Ephesian elders that he is innocent of the blood of all because he has not shrunk from declaring to them "the whole counsel of God." The term here translated as "counsel" (βουλή/*boulē*) can also be rendered "will," "purpose," or even "plan," and when it is linked with God it is very important in Luke and Acts (occurring for the first time in Luke 7:30, as well as in Acts 13:36, part of Paul's first reported sermon; see also Acts 2:23; 4:28). Used in this way, *boulē* often has echoes of Scripture's revealing of God's great plan of redemption, which finds its focus in the necessary death and resurrection of Jesus, and which results in the evangelization of all nations (cf. Rom. 16:25–26). It is apparent then that "declaring . . . the . . . counsel of God" is somewhat parallel to "testify[ing] to the gospel of the grace of God" and "proclaiming the kingdom" in the preceding verses (Acts 20:24, 25). It is also similar to Paul's idea of the "will of our God" (Gal. 1:4; cf. Eph. 1:3–14) and his outline of God's purposes in his letter to the Romans (chaps. 1–6).

But the idea is even fuller in our passage, being modified by "the whole" (πᾶς; πᾶσαν τὴν βουλὴν / *pas*; *pasan tēn boulēn*). This means that Paul does not just give the Ephesians a summary, overview, or highlights package of God's plans, but rather that he carefully instructs them in the complete counsel of God as it is available to him. This accords well with the fact that Ephesus has been the headquarters of Paul's work in Asia Minor for two to three years (Acts 19:10; 20:31) and that he has devoted his time there to "teaching . . . in public and from house to house" (20:20). It also squares with the fact that prior to Paul's arrival, the believers in Ephesus had received only a piecemeal teaching of the faith, having been formed well on some important matters, but not on others (18:24–19:7). They needed "the *whole* counsel of God" to be ministered to them in order to reach maturity in the faith.

It is also important to see that in our passage, Paul is passing the baton to the elders of Ephesus. He is not simply reminiscing about his ministry with them, but is reminding them of his model of ministry so that they can take it up and continue where he leaves off. Paul knows that he will not return to minister among them again (Acts 20:25) but that others will come with the intention of destroying the church, and that the best protection for the flock of God under the care of the Ephesian elders is the word of God (v. 32; cf. vv. 25–32), the whole counsel of God (v. 27).

In summary, Acts 20:17–38 shows that it is the duty of church leaders to preach the whole counsel of God as Paul did, with the person and work of Jesus at the center, and a commitment to expound everything that God has revealed through his word. This focus on Christ and attention to the breadth of Scripture is captured in the disciplines that we will later talk about as biblical theology and gospel theology, those being approaches to each and every part of the Bible that maintain perspective on the whole plan, purpose, or will of God that is ultimately fulfilled in and focused on his Son.

## All Scripture Is God-Breathed and Useful (2 Tim. 3)

The second passage that frames our approach to preaching the whole Bible is 2 Timothy 3:10–17. Like Acts 20:17–38, it is a leadership charge, but this time to one individual, Paul's protégé Timothy. There are a number of things to note about what Paul says. First, he again points to his own teaching and conduct, which is the pattern that he calls Timothy to imitate (2 Tim. 3:10–11, 14). Second, he notes the context of persecution, which should be expected for all in ministry and which is coupled with some people's aim of distorting the truth (vv. 12–13). The implication is that the truth needs to be taught rightly. After this, Paul reminds Timothy of his good foundation in the "sacred writings" (v. 15), and this leads Paul into his comments about the nature and power of the written word of God (vv. 15–17).

In the first instance, he reminds Timothy that the Scriptures are able to make people wise for salvation through faith in Christ Jesus (2 Tim. 3:15). In other words, it is as people faithfully receive the words of the Old Testament Scriptures—that is, the word of

God—that they hear about Jesus. As these words are received, people are saved. This is saying something parallel to, and something converse to, Acts 20:27. In that text, we saw that people need the whole counsel of God, not the bare minimum necessary to get them saved. Here we see that the sacred writings as a whole instruct people in the ways of salvation in Christ—that is, they point to the central message of Jesus as Savior and Lord of all. Interestingly, this is as true of the Old Testament as of the New. Of course, at the time when Paul wrote to Timothy, there was no written New Testament, and so "sacred writings" refers to just the Jewish Scriptures and possibly a few of the early apostolic texts that would later become part of the New Testament. Yet we know from passages such as John 5:39–40 that even the Old Testament Scriptures, when correctly interpreted, bear witness to Jesus and are intended to bring their readers to him to receive eternal life. As we noted above, our theological frameworks are essential to us seeing every part of Scripture fold into the grand story at its center, the saving work of Jesus.

As he continues in 2 Timothy 3:16–17, which again parallel Acts 20:27, Paul does not just speak about "Scripture," but about "*all* Scripture" (πᾶσα γραφὴ / *pasa graphē*), and says that it is all "breathed out by God." This is a relatively direct way of saying that every word written—or inscripturated—in the Bible is a word spoken from God. That is, it is not just those parts of the Bible that record direct quotations from God that are to be regarded as the word of God, but the entire text of the Scriptures. Given this statement, we probably cannot imagine Paul being very enthusiastic about red-letter Bibles, which give us the words of Jesus in red, perhaps to indicate their particular divine nature compared with the other words in the Bible. Instead, Paul knows that *every* word in the Bible is divinely inspired—even expirated—and so all must be respected and embraced as such.

What Paul is saying here aligns with Jesus's own respect for the whole Bible as the word of God, captured in his ongoing commitment to its every iota and dot (Matt. 5:18).[3] Although most Christians are familiar with the idea of the Bible as the word of God, this is still quite a profound notion. In the first instance, it of course means that we do not dismiss any part of the Bible, and neither do we add to it, as though our words could stand beside God's. In addition to this baseline conviction about the scope of God's word, we may also need to think about the nature of God's word. God's words to us are not only in the form of direct address, but also come as genealogies, laws, stories, philosophical reflections, poems, letters to churches, and more. We must also recognize odd things, such as that those parts of the Bible that are addressed *to* God, as are many of the psalms, are also words for us *from* God. All of this is Scripture, and it is all the breathed-out words of God.

Paul's statement about the inspiration of Scripture is made on the way to another point, which is that if the Scriptures have their source in God, then they are "profitable" or "useful" (2 Tim. 3:16). This usefulness is expanded in the four terms that follow: *teaching, reproof, correction,* and *training in righteousness.* The pattern of these four aspects of Scripture's usefulness is chiastic, with the first and the last having to do with education, and the second and third having to do with identifying and correcting sin. This neatly balances the facts that Scripture has a *positively educative* function that addresses both doctrine and ethics, as well as a *corrective* function also directed at doctrine and ethics. The ultimate goal is that "the man of God [possibly referring to the church pastor, or possibly just an archaic way of saying "every person of God"] may be complete, equipped for every good work" (v. 17). Once more we see that teaching and learning the Bible is not just an end in and of itself, but is also a means of formation for people who will actively live their lives to the glory of God and for the benefit of others.

---

3. *Iota* is a letter of the Greek alphabet and is small, written as just a short line (ι). The fact that Jesus talked about Scripture containing *iotas* shows that he was familiar with the Greek version of the Old Testament, now known to scholars as the Septuagint.

If this nature, character, and purpose of Scripture is extended to the entire New Testament as well as the Old, as we believe it is, we could summarize by saying that the Bible *as a whole* is the word of God and has the goal of making those who receive it wise for salvation through faith in Christ Jesus, and that *every text* of the Bible is useful for keeping believers straight in terms of doctrine and ethics, and for enabling pastor-teachers such as Timothy to keep their people straight in the same. The implications of this for preaching are profound. We must preach the Scriptures in the way that they were designed. A full view of Jesus comes only from a full examination of the testimony to him in all of the Scriptures. Moreover, a full view of how to think about and live the Christian life also comes only from a full examination of all the texts of Scripture. It follows that our congregations must be fed on as much of Scripture as is possible through our preaching.

## What Is Preaching Anyway?

The practical purpose of this book is to help preachers follow through on the basic theological conviction about the whole of the Bible being God's word to his world by actually working to preach the whole Bible to the people they minister among. We want to assist in bridging the gap between what evangelical Christians commonly declare to be true and their actual week-to-week practice. However, before we go any further, we must pause to provide some clarity around what we mean by preaching, because this is not, in fact, a straightforward biblical word, and neither are many common ideas about preaching drawn directly from the Scriptures.

When we find the word *preach* (and its various cognates) in our English New Testaments, it is usually a translation of one of two words in the original Greek. The first of those words is *euangelizo* (εὐαγγελίζω), which is a verb meaning "to gospel" or "gospelling," or alternatively "to good news" or "good newsing" ("good news" being the literal meaning of *gospel*). These are somewhat clunky terms in English because we are more used to the words *gospel* and *news* being nouns. For this reason, our English translations often render *euangelizo* as "bring the gospel/ good news" (e.g., Luke 1:19; Acts 13:32), "proclaim the gospel/ good news" (e.g., Luke 4:18), or "*preach* the gospel/good news" (e.g., Matt. 11:5; Luke 3:18; Acts 8:12). These are all smooth and appropriate ways to translate *euangelizo* in modern English and, importantly, they retain its emphasis on evangelistic proclamation.

However, things are a little more ambiguous when *euangelizo* is translated as just "preach" or "preaching" without "the gospel" or "the good news" included. In some cases, this is necessary, as the English would simply be too clunky for a fuller translation. For example, in the ESV, Acts 8:4 says,

> Now those who were scattered went about preaching the word [εὐαγγελιζόμενοι τὸν λόγον / *euangelizomenoi ton logon*].

This is a reasonable translation, because it is hard to think how "gospel" as a noun could be worked in; trying to do so woodenly would result in something like this:

> Now those who were scattered went about preaching the gospel, the word.

If *gospel* and *word* refer to the same thing here, this would be not only bad English, but also unnecessary.[4] But there is a problem that results when we have only "preaching the word" in English, because with this phrasing, we risk losing the evangelistic sense implicit in the original *euangelizo*. Because of our cultural history, we now too easily read "preaching the word" as "teaching the word to believers," or even as "delivering half-hour

---

4. Different English translations of the Bible deal with this verse differently. The King James Version, the New International Version, and the New American Standard Version all have "preached/preaching," but the New Revised Standard Version has "proclaiming" and the Contemporary English Version has "telling." The New English Translation even has "proclaiming the good news of the word," which is admirable in its inclusion of "good news," although it only manages this by also inserting "of."

expository monologues in a Sunday morning church service." That is to say, in today's Western Christian culture, we do not immediately understand *preach* as just "evangelize." Of course, we do have a mental category for evangelistic preaching, where the good news of Jesus is presented in a well-prepared talk directed to unbelievers, but we tend to think of evangelistic preaching as a subcategory of preaching. For most of us, when we think of preaching, our minds quickly go to a pastor delivering a message from the platform of a Christian church as part of a formal weekly service. But again, this is not the meaning of the word *euangelizo*, and so when it is simply translated as "preach" in our New Testaments, our baggage brings more to that text than the text itself gives to us. Because of this, it would probably be better if *euangelizo* was regularly translated as "proclaim" in our Bibles, as we do tend to more naturally connect the idea of proclamation with evangelism. If this had been done for our Acts 8:4 text in the ESV, it would read:

> Now those who were scattered went about proclaiming the word.

This reads well in English, and also makes clearer that the scattered believers went out evangelizing (as the rest of Acts 8 begins to detail), not just explaining the Bible to each other.

The second word that is sometimes translated as "preach" in our English Bibles is *kēryssō* (κηρύσσω), although of its sixty-one occurrences, the ESV renders it this way only seventeen times. For all but one of the other instances, it is translated as "proclaim," which again gives the sense that it may be referring to an evangelistic activity.[5] In fact, a good case can be made for "proclaim" as the preferred translation of *kēryssō* because it sometimes occurs as part of the larger phrases *kēryssō to euangelion* (κηρύσσω τὸ εὐαγγέλιον, meaning "proclaim the gospel," e.g., Matt. 4:23; 9:35; Mark 1:14); *kēryssō tēn basileian* (κηρύσσω

---

5. The other instance of *kēryssō* in the ESV (Mark 1:45) is translated as "talk."

τὴν βασιλείαν, meaning "proclaim the kingdom," e.g., Luke 9:2; Acts 20:25); *kēryssō ton logon* (κηρύσσω τὸν λόγον, meaning "proclaim the message," e.g., 2 Tim. 4:2 NRSV); *kēryssō Christon estaurōmenon* (κηρύσσω Χριστὸν ἐσταυρωμένον, meaning "proclaim Christ crucified," e.g., 1 Cor. 1:23 NRSV); or just *kēryssō ton Iēsoun* (κηρύσσω τὸν Ἰησοῦν, meaning "proclaim Jesus," e.g., Acts 9:20). In all of those cases, it is clear that an evangelistic activity is being reported, and that meaning is not lost even if *kēryssō* is translated as "preach"—that would simply read "preach the gospel/kingdom/etc." A study of all of the instances of *kēryssō* on its own suggests that most often it is really just standing as a shorthand for the fuller phrases that talk about evangelistic activity. This means that it seems best if both *euangelizo* and *kēryssō* are generally translated as "proclaim" throughout the New Testament. Therefore, as a rule of thumb, we recommend mentally substituting "proclaim" or "preach the gospel" each time we see "preach" in our English Bibles. In most cases, this will better reflect the underlying meaning.

What does all this mean for our preaching? Should we, in fact, not seek to systematically expound the Scriptures to church members at all, but just redirect all of our energies to evangelistic preaching? While it would be no bad thing at all to grow our evangelistic activities, we do not think that the lack of overlap between the words *euangelizo* and *kēryssō*, and what we had often understood preaching to be—pulpit ministry—means that we should not bother working to preach through the whole Bible to believers. This is simply because the New Testament talks of more than just evangelism; it also has a strong emphasis on *teaching* (διδάσκω/*didaskō*) the Bible, and teaching in the New Testament does largely seem to be an activity directed toward believers (e.g., Matt. 4:23; Mark 1:21; Luke 4:15; John 6:59; Acts 4:2; Rom. 2:21; 1 Cor. 4:17; etc.). Given that sometimes sermons can be both for teaching believers and for evangelism (something we will discuss more in chap. 12), and given that much teaching and much evangelism is not done via sermons, we can helpfully diagram the relationship between evangelism, teaching, and what we know as preaching as follows:

Fig. 1.1. Evangelism, Teaching, and Preaching.

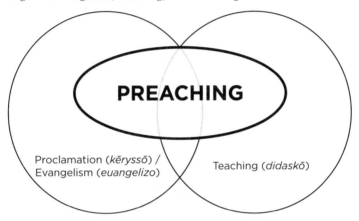

We are comfortable knowing that what we tend to think of as preaching is not the only possible way of fulfilling what the New Testament calls for in evangelizing and teaching. Additionally, we think that extensive works of evangelism and Bible teaching could—and should—happen apart from the preacher's weekly sermons. In fact, theoretically, we believe it could be possible for a church to be faithful to the Bible's call to evangelize and preach without any pulpit ministry whatsoever. However, we also believe that preaching as we know it has become a great tradition of the church over the centuries precisely because it is an excellent means for both evangelism and teaching. There are several reasons why this is the case.

First, preaching is a highly efficient way to teach many people at the same time. Hundreds, and even thousands, can receive a sermon all at once, meaning that huge economies of effort are possible in preaching. This, in turn, means that preachers are able to give more time to preaching more parts of the Bible. Second, and following on, preaching has the power to shape whole communities of God's people as members of local churches all hear a common message. The corporate mind and will can be addressed in preaching as the preacher brings God's word to a gathered fellowship of faith, and not just to many people individually. This is critical for the healthy common life of a body of believers. Finally, preaching enables the development of a sustained, detailed, and well-crafted message that is meaningfully connected to previous and following messages. Dialogue with individuals or groups can have a tendency to wander from one topic to the next depending on the particular questions and priorities of those involved. Pedagogically, this is both good and bad. It is good because people are more likely to absorb information if they are engaged as conversation partners and get to chase down their own interests. But it can also be a problem because if people are prioritizing their own interests and questions in conversations, they may be less likely to allow the word of God to set the agenda and come to them uninterrupted. Even some of the best group Bible studies have a tendency to drift from topic to topic rather than tightly following a single passage of Scripture from start to finish. But a sermon—like any good prepared speech—can be carefully focused and can deliver an integrated message that has been thoroughly thought through from start to finish.

For all of these reasons, we believe that preaching sermons—expository monologues—is perhaps the single best way to work toward feeding the people of God with the word of God in its entirety.

## 2

# The Canon of Scripture

Given that all Scripture is inspired by God and is useful for teaching, for reproof, for correction, and for training in righteousness, the obvious question is, What should be counted as Scripture? At one level, the answer is straightforward and nowadays assumed among like-minded mainstream Protestant Christians. By "Scripture," we mean the Christian Bible as it is commonly published, in its various translations, as a collection of sixty-six books spanning the two Testaments. And—to preempt our conclusion—we believe that this assumption is indeed good and worthy, and based on sound theology, history, and reasoning.

Below is a brief overview of how the church has come to its settled position on the scope and contents of the canon (meaning "rule," or regulated collection) of Scripture. We will consider both the internal evidence of the Bible itself, as well as some of the relevant history.[1] Following this, we will give a brief overview of the ways that the books of the Bible can be grouped, something that will become important when we start thinking about how to plan preaching programs.

---

1. For a fuller discussion of canon, see Lee Martin McDonald, *The Biblical Canon: Its Origin, Transmission, and Authority* (Peabody, MA: Hendrickson, 2007), 80ff., 190ff.

## Jesus and the New Testament on the Old Testament

In several places in the Gospels, we see Jesus engaging parts of the Jewish Scriptures—what we now call the Old Testament—and these incidents teach us a great deal. It is quite clear that Jesus's default position is that these Jewish Scriptures are the true, unchangeable, and authoritative word of God. This assumption is primarily seen in the way Jesus calls on and uses these Scriptures in his ministry. For example, in Luke 4:1–13, Jesus rebuts Satan's tests by quoting from Deuteronomy and prefacing each of his responses with the simple statement "It is written" or "It is said." For Jesus, whatever stands written in that part of the Jewish Scriptures is the definitive and binding word of God, and it is determinative for his own convictions and decision making. In the incident following this wilderness testing (vv. 16–21), Jesus is in the synagogue at Nazareth, where he reads publicly from the prophet Isaiah. And while his comment on the passage he has read is confronting for his audience—Jesus claims that *he* embodies the fulfillment of Isaiah's prophecy—his conviction about the nature of Isaiah's written prophecy is the same as that of the other Jews in the synagogue: it is the God-given and authoritative "Scripture" (v. 21). Therefore, within just a single chapter of Luke's Gospel, we see that Jesus considers two different parts of what we now call the Old Testament to be Scripture.

From here, we would naturally ask whether Jesus's view extends to the rest of the Old Testament, and this would seem to be likely. By the first century, the Jewish Scriptures were a reasonably well-defined collection of works, and every contemporary Jew would have known that Deuteronomy and Isaiah were part of that collection. Indeed, the authority of those two books (or scrolls, as they would have been at the time) was recognized partly by virtue of their being in the collection.

The collection of the Jewish Scriptures was, in fact, broken into three main parts. The first was the Torah, or "Law of Moses," sometimes just called the "Law" or even just "Moses" for short (e.g., Luke 16:29). It was comprised of the first five books of our Old Testament, Genesis through Deuteronomy—hence the fact that Bible translators and scholars now also give these books the collective title the "Pentateuch," meaning "five scrolls." These books begin by recounting the creation of the world and of human beings, who demonstrate themselves to be sinful and are therefore banished from God's presence. The call of Abraham and the promises made to him in chapter 12:1–3 then have the restoration and blessing of all humanity in focus. After tracing the story of Abraham's family in Genesis 12–50, the rest of the Pentateuch recounts the history of the people of Israel from their time as slaves in Egypt through their deliverance and extended wilderness wanderings, with the giving of the Law, the establishment of religious practices, and censuses, right up to the point where the people were stationed on the verge of the promised land.

The second part of the Jewish Scriptures was the "Prophets," and it included the historical books from Joshua through Kings; the three Major Prophets, Isaiah, Jeremiah, and Ezekiel; and the twelve Minor Prophets. These texts record the story of Israel from its entry into the promised land through the establishment of the monarchy and on to the long decline of the nation, including its division into the two subkingdoms of Israel and Judah, which were eventually defeated by Assyria and Babylon respectively. A number of the prophets were from these times, while others were from the later period when Israel returned from its exile in Babylon and was partially reestablished in the promised land.

The third part of the Jewish Scriptures was the "Writings," and although we are not sure that its contents were as tightly defined as the Law and Prophets in the first century, it included texts such as the Psalms, Proverbs, and Job; the five small works of Ruth, Esther, Ecclesiastes, Song of Solomon, and Lamentations; the histories in the books of Chronicles, Ezra, and Nehemiah; and the book of Daniel. There is great variety in these writings, with more of the history of Israel, spanning from the time of the judges to the restoration after the exile, and then some poetry and works of wisdom, mostly from the time of the monarchy.

In the New Testament, in the many cases where the Law, or the Law of Moses, is spoken of, the reference is to the whole collection of the first five books. One clear example of this comes in Mark 12:26, where Jesus refers the Sadducees to the "book of Moses," in the singular, and what it says about the flaming bush, an incident found in Exodus 3. There are also a number of cases in the New Testament where the Law of Moses and the Prophets are referred to as a pair, and this is probably a shorthand way of referring to the entire Jewish Scriptures (e.g., Matt. 5:17; 7:12; 22:40; Luke 16:29–31; John 1:45; Acts 28:23). That this is the case is demonstrated in Luke 24:27, where the risen Jesus interprets the whole Scriptures "beginning with Moses and all the Prophets," with the two named collections naturally leading on to a consideration of the entire Scriptures. Similarly, in verse 44 of the same chapter, Jesus reminds his disciples that "everything written about me in the Law of Moses and the Prophets and the Psalms must be fulfilled." Here, Jesus may be taking "the Psalms" as shorthand for all of the Writings, perhaps confirmed in verse 45, which says that he "opened their minds to understand the Scriptures," meaning the Scriptures as a whole.

In addition to these examples, Jesus's endorsement of the Jewish Scriptures in their entirety is perhaps most famously known from Matthew 5:17–19, at the start of his Sermon on the Mount, where he says,

> Do not think that I have come to abolish the Law or the Prophets; I have not come to abolish them but to fulfill them. For truly, I say to you, until heaven and earth pass away, not an iota, not a dot, will pass from the Law until all is accomplished. Therefore whoever relaxes one of the least of these commandments and teaches others to do the same will be called least in the kingdom of heaven, but whoever does them and teaches them will be called great in the kingdom of heaven.

All of this shows that what we now call the Old Testament was both quite well established and considered to be authoritative Scripture by God's people, and by Jesus himself, in New Testament times.

## The New Testament on the New Testament

Second Peter 3:15–16 says,

> And count the patience of our Lord as salvation, just as our beloved brother Paul also wrote to you according to the wisdom given him, as he does in all his letters when he speaks in them of these matters. There are some things in them that are hard to understand, which the ignorant and unstable twist to their own destruction, as they do the other Scriptures.

This is a remarkable passage because it shows that the early Christians not only followed Jesus in upholding the Jewish Scriptures, but that they had also started to take additional writings as Scripture, in this case, Paul's letters. But while this was a very significant development, it is perhaps not too surprising. Since the early church considered Jesus to be the Messiah, it follows that they would take very seriously those things written about him by his appointed spokesmen, the apostles.

We again see this kind of dedication to the apostles' teachings in Acts 2:42, which says,

> And they [members of the early church] devoted themselves to the apostles' teaching and the fellowship, to the breaking of bread and the prayers.

It is not clear that the apostles' teaching had been preserved in writing at this stage; the early church could have been committed to the apostles' words as they were passed on verbally. But this would not change the point that the first Christians considered the words of Jesus's apostles to be central to their understanding and practice of their faith.

Going a step further back, we see that the apostles wrote only what they considered to be in accord with the teaching of Jesus, and in some cases they closely echo, or even directly quote, his teaching as it is now recorded in the Gospels. For example, in 1 Corinthians 11:23–26, Paul says, "For I received from the Lord what I also delivered to you," before going on to quote Jesus's words from Luke 22:19–20. Similarly, in 1 Corinthians 15:1–5, the gospel that Paul has received and passed on lines up very neatly with Jesus's own teaching in places such as Mark 8:31 (and many others). And in 2 Corinthians 1:17–20, Paul is clearly drawing on Jesus's teaching from Matthew 5:33–37. While it is true that most of the apostles' writings cannot be connected so directly to the recorded words of Jesus, it is nonetheless certainly the case that the apostles' special understanding of Jesus as Messiah and Savior is unambiguously central in all of their preserved works.

And of course, behind all of this lies the most basic Christian belief—that Jesus is the one who most fully reveals the truth about God, supplying even more than Moses and the Prophets. This is explicitly affirmed in the New Testament in places such as John 1:17–18, which says,

> For the law was given through Moses; grace and truth came through Jesus Christ. No one has ever seen God; the only God, who is at the Father's side, he has made him known.

Likewise, Matthew 11:25–27 says,

> At that time Jesus declared, "I thank you, Father, Lord of heaven and earth, that you have hidden these things from the wise and understanding and revealed them to little children; yes, Father, for such was your gracious will. All things have been handed over to me by my Father, and no one knows the Son except the Father, and no one knows the Father except the Son and anyone to whom the Son chooses to reveal him."

Again, Hebrews 1:1–2a says,

Long ago, at many times and in many ways, God spoke to our
fathers by the prophets, but in these last days he has spoken
to us by his Son.

This commitment to the revelation of Jesus himself and to the
teaching of his endorsed apostles explains why many of the writings in the New Testament came to be understood as Scripture.

There is, however, still a fair question of whether this adequately accounts for the entirety of the New Testament. The first
thing to note in this connection is that more of the New Testament
has been recognized to have apostolic connections than might be
initially apparent. Matthew, John, Paul, and Peter are easily recognized as apostles, and together, their writings make up around
60 percent of the New Testament. Apart from these writings are
the works of Mark, Luke, the anonymous author of the letter (or
perhaps sermon) to the Hebrews, James, and Jude. Mark is commonly thought to have drawn much of what he includes in his
Gospel from Peter, and Luke is known to have been very close to
Paul (the switch to "we" language in Acts 16, 20–21 and 27–28
shows that Luke, the author of that book, was with Paul at these
times. See also 2 Tim. 4:11.) Therefore, Mark's Gospel, Luke's
Gospel, and Acts can be reasonably thought of as apostolic at one
remove. Then, for much of church history (although not so commonly today), the letter to the Hebrews was thought to have been
written by Paul and so was naturally included in the New Testament. That leaves only the letters of James and Jude, which have
indeed been among the most disputed New Testament books with
regard to their canonicity. However, both of the authors of these
letters also claim an exceptionally close connection to Jesus: they
are thought to have been his biological brothers (i.e., natural sons
of Joseph and Mary born after Jesus; see Matt. 13:55–56; Mark
6:3; Gal. 1:19; Jude 1). Even if these close connections to Jesus
are not all completely certain, the likelihood of them again shows
that the early church prioritized the writings of those people who

were most intimately connected to him when considering what it ought to receive as Scripture.

Beyond these authorial credentials, the character of the writings was also very important to the early church. It is not by accident that all of the books of the New Testament are focused on Jesus and address the life of his followers or those who are being presented with his message. The first Christians were not interested in simply gathering anything that the apostles wrote (for example, their more private letters or shopping lists), but just those writings that were intended by them to communicate to others the faith they held (cf. John 20:30–31).

## Formalization of the New Testament Canon

The best way to think of the formalization of the New Testament is in terms of recognition rather than sanction. That is, it is not that the believers in the earliest church decided that they wanted a Bible and therefore went about establishing an official set of criteria that they could use to determine whether or not various texts should be included in it and thus granted the status of Scripture. Neither did they go about imposing any such criteria on a wide variety of texts that had not formerly been of any prominence among them. Rather, it was that they first began reading and circulating the various apostolic, Jesus-centric documents, and then, after those documents had been generally accepted as authoritative by the churches for a considerable time, formally recognized them as such. So having received the letters sent to them by the apostles, the written accounts of Jesus's life, and the other New Testament writings, the first Christians began to share them with each other, as indeed some of those texts directed them to do (e.g., Col. 4:16; 1 Thess. 5:27; Rev. 1:3). In time, many copies of these writings were made and bound together into what we might call proto-New Testaments, although these collections had no formally established and accepted table of contents for the first generations of the church.

After this, there were several points at which formalization occurred. One of the early and famous moments was in the second century, when a certain Marcion from Pontus (a region in Asia Minor, modern-day Turkey) decided to significantly narrow down the list of books that he would consider Scripture to only those that would support his particular views of Jesus and God the Father. It was in response to this that the leaders of the early church began compiling their own formal lists of New Testament books that better reflected their long-standing traditions of acceptance. There was some variation in those early lists, but much agreement had been reached by the late fourth century, and so it was relatively easy to come to a general consensus about the canon.

In the fourth century, soon after Christianity had become the state religion of the Roman Empire, a Latin translation of all of the texts generally accepted as Scripture, both Old and New Testaments, was made by the priest Jerome. This became known as the Vulgate because it was in the universally common, or "vulgar," imperial tongue. While there were always other versions of the Scriptures, in the Middle Ages, Jerome's compilation became the primary approved Bible of the Roman Catholic Church, and therefore of the Western world—and it remained so right through to the Renaissance and the Protestant Reformation, as noted in the introduction. This meant that Jerome's canon was considered *the* canon for the church in the West up until the sixteenth century, and indeed it was in the sixteenth century that the Council of Trent turned this tradition into doctrine for the Roman Catholic Church.

The good news in this is that all of the books that later scholarship has recognized as being either apostolic or accepted as Scripture by the early church were included in the Vulgate. However, the Vulgate also included the books that Protestant Christians consider to be apocryphal. These are books that can be found in the early Greek translations of the Old Testament, but not in the

Hebrew Scriptures; they were additional to the established Jewish collections of the Law, Prophets, and Writings. In fact, one of the reasons that the early Protestant movement was considered to be so subversive to Rome was not just that it was reclaiming the Scriptures for the people by translating them into the native languages of Europe, but also that it was separating out the apocryphal books from the Old Testament and openly questioning their canonicity. Ultimately, this would become one of the major dividing lines between Roman Catholics and Protestants, and still today, the former include the apocryphal books in their Bibles while the latter do not.

It is important to note that, in addition to these books' pedigree in the Old Testament, something that Jerome himself questioned, the Protestants were also very troubled by parts of the Apocrypha that contain teachings that are nigh impossible to reconcile with the New Testament. For example, the core Roman Catholic doctrine of purgatory finds its best justification in the apocryphal book 2 Maccabees, but it is very hard to defend from just the Old and New Testaments, and indeed clashes with points they clearly teach about justification. We believe that the Protestant judgments were correct, and so we do not include the Apocrypha in either our understanding of the canon of Scripture or in our preaching programs. Ultimately, we do not believe that it is the word of God, and therefore do not think it ought to be treated as though it were. We do think, however, that the Apocrypha is worth reading for the historical light it casts on the intertestamental period, and for the awareness it brings to some of the beliefs, customs, and writing conventions of the first-century Jews whom we meet in the New Testament.

In addition to knowing about the Apocrypha, it is also important to recognize that there are, in fact, some other parts of our common English Bibles that should not be considered Scripture. These include the so-called shorter and longer endings of Mark's Gospel (Mark 16:8b, 9–20), the "sweating blood" verse (Luke

22:44), and the story of the woman caught committing adultery (John 7:53–8:11). Despite the long tradition of including these texts in the Bible, they are all now recognized to be late additions and not part of the original texts of the books into which they have been inserted. Most modern English Bibles flag the dubious nature of these passages with footnotes or with brackets around the passages, but it is quite a shame that old habits have prevailed over good scholarship such that we continue to have these extra passages spliced into the original Scriptures in most of our translations. Certainly it is worth keeping an eye on your Bible's footnotes for this kind of thing.

Finally, it is worth noting at this point that the newer translations of the Bible tend to be more accurate than the older, which is exactly what we would expect to find as the discipline of biblical translation continues to advance over time. Therefore, even though many Christians love the King James Version of 1611 for its lovely English prose and classic turns of phrase, it needs to be recognized as a translation that has some errors that have been corrected in more modern translations. For example, when the heavenly host appears to the shepherds in Luke 2:14 and praises God, the King James Version has the angels saying, "Glory to God in the highest, and on earth peace, good will toward men." Newer translations, however, have recognized that there was, in fact, one additional letter in one word of the original Greek text that stands behind this verse. Accounting for the change that letter makes (εὐδοκία/eudokia → εὐδοκίας/eudokias, which makes "good will"/"pleasure" not the subject of the clause, but a quality of those to whom peace is directed), the more modern translations render the verse as "Glory to God in the highest, and on earth peace among those with *whom he is pleased!*" or similar. Clearly there is a difference of meaning that results. In the King James Version, we could be led to believe that the heavenly host are declaring God's good will toward all people (assuming that "men" is being used in its old-fashioned way to stand for men and women).

The newer translations, however, make it clear that God's peace is a gift of his special grace toward those people who have found his favor. Needless to say, we recommend preaching from a modern translation of the Bible that is grounded in the most up-to-date textual scholarship to avoid any unnecessary problems.

# 3

# Failing to Preach the Whole Bible

Most Bible-believing Christians, and certainly most Bible-teaching pastors, probably would not have found too much to disagree with in the previous chapters. We evangelicals believe that the whole of Scripture is the word of God to the people of his world. We believe that the standard Protestant Bible, with its thirty-nine Old Testament books and twenty-seven New Testament books, is no more than and no less than the fullness of the Scriptures. And we believe, at least in principle, that the entirety of the Bible should be taught to all believers, and even offered to those who aren't yet followers of Jesus. But as noted in the introduction, we all also know that too few churches make any serious attempt to actually teach or preach through the whole Bible. In fact, we would likely be quite taken aback (in a good way) to hear of a church that was following a plan to achieve this monumental task.

Before we start sharing some frameworks and outlining an approach to help more preachers work toward this worthy goal, we will use this chapter to explore what preaching looks like in many churches that do not actively seek to teach the whole Bible, and what some of the consequences of this are. Our hope in this is simply that preachers will recognize what preaching ministries look like when they offer less than the whole Bible, understand their shortcomings and risks, and thereby be strengthened in their resolve to commit to bringing as much of God's word to his people as possible.

## Why Don't We Preach the Whole Bible?

Given all that we have considered so far, the obvious question arises again: Why on earth wouldn't every church seek to preach through the whole Bible? There are a few very obvious and very good answers to it, and we will come to those. Being honest, though, the first answer may be that some of us never have actually thought about the question very much. Like so many preachers, the two of us took time to ensure that we were well trained to preach biblically faithful sermons, but we were never taught anything much at all about preaching *series* of sermons, let alone constructing a program of preaching that would move through the entire Bible. In fact, few seminaries teach anything about designing preaching programs, even though many have a strong emphasis on preacher training. Pastors tend to think about these things more in the years after seminary, when they become senior leaders of churches with the responsibility not just for the preaching, but also for planning the preaching too. At that point, many just adopt a pattern similar to that which they saw their own pastors following in the past without giving extended thought as to whether it should be changed, or how they might make the changes.

We would be remiss not to mention at this point that there are, in fact, many churches that have inherited a very strong tradition of paying attention to the Bible as a whole. Some of these are the churches that have retained the use of a lectionary or other program of seriatim Bible reading. The Church of England, for example, has a relatively comprehensive lectionary in its authoritative Book of Common Prayer, which continues to be the source of much Anglican liturgy around the world today. This lectionary outlines a public Bible-reading plan that takes the church through the Old Testament once every year, the New Testament twice per year, and the Psalms once per month. This is an incredibly rich diet of Scripture.

Even so, the Anglican lectionary was established as a public Bible-reading plan, so it has shortcomings when used as a preaching schedule. One is that it does not actually cover the whole Protestant Bible, but leaves out various passages for various reasons, and even includes some readings from the Apocrypha. Another is that it assumes readings will be done twice a day, not just once a week in church, meaning that churches that meet only for a single Sunday service would end up preaching only from every seventh reading, which would be a very unhelpful staccato approach to the Scriptures. Finally, less than one in seven set readings actually would be preached by following this lectionary, as it offers multiple readings for each day, and these are not necessarily related to one another in any specific way. This, of course, means that a preacher would have to choose one of the readings as the focus of his sermon, unless he were to attempt the almost impossible task of preaching a coherent sermon from all of the set readings each week. The bottom line with this lectionary, and most others, is that while it may be a good daily reading guide, it is probably not helpful for charting a weekly preaching program that seeks to teach the whole Bible to a congregation.

Thinking about lectionaries does help us realize more of the practical challenges in preaching the whole Bible. Even for those of us who have recognized and embraced the ideal, the basic truth is that we find it hard to imagine how we could possibly manage the practicalities, as the task might seem completely overwhelming. The Bible takes a long time to read, let alone preach through. When we start thinking about that, we know we cannot be working with time frames of just weeks or months, but need to be considering what we will do for years *or even decades*.

In addition to the practical issues, other questions that we may struggle with come to the surface when we consider preaching *every part* of Scripture. What would we do with those parts of the Old Testament that seem to ban things we find acceptable, such as eating pork, or endorse things we might find immoral, such as holy war (e.g., Lev. 11:7; Deut. 20:10–18)? What about those parts of the Bible that seem to give rise to so much conflict in the church, such as its teaching on gender and gender roles (e.g., Eph. 5:22–33; 1 Tim. 2:8–15)? Then there are the parts that simply don't make quick sense to us, such as Paul discussing baptism on behalf of the dead (1 Cor. 15:29) or Peter talking about Jesus's proclamation to the spirits in prison after his death (1 Pet. 3:18–20). And, of course, we know that there seem to be inconsistencies or even contradictions in the Bible, a good example being Jesus teaching "Whoever is not with me is against me" (Matt. 12:30) *and* "The one who is not against us is for us" (Mark 9:40). On top of these issues there are the parts of the Bible that, being honest, we just can't see the value in, such as some of the long slabs of Old Testament narrative (e.g., the accounts of the kingly reigns in 1–2 Kings) or the New Testament genealogies (e.g., Matt. 1:1–16), which might appear to be interesting to a particular type of historian, but of little help to rank-and-file believers. Lastly, there are the challenges in facing not only the workload that would be created by preaching through the whole Bible, but also those parts of the Scriptures that we find personally confronting, unsettling, or convicting (e.g., Ps. 137:7–9 or the language used about God as enemy in Lamentations 2). In agreeing to engage the whole Bible, we realize that we are opening up not just our congregations, but even ourselves, to be examined by all of God's word. Nonetheless, even as we acknowledge these challenges, all this is as it should be for those entrusted with the high calling of teaching and pastoring Jesus's flock. It is a difficult work.

Many of the issues flagged above will be addressed in the pages that follow, with some encouragement on how they might be dealt with. First, however, we will give some examples of what it looks like to *not* preach the whole Bible.

## What It Looks Like

Preaching that does not work through the whole Bible can look different in different churches and ministries. At worst, a church could have no preaching or teaching of the Bible at all. This might mean no teaching of any kind—as might be the case in some very liturgically focused churches—or teaching that does not attempt to explain or apply the Scriptures, but rather seeks to convey other ideas or messages. It is actually possible that some churches could employ these practices with some good intentions. They may have concluded that teaching the Bible is too alienating for the unchurched people they are trying to reach; too complicated for congregations that just want practical advice for living; or even too simplistic for their more sophisticated members. But even with motivations such as these, we are of the view that a nonbiblical ministry is ultimately a sub-Christian ministry. Moreover, we believe that preaching God's words in the Bible will do far more to achieve a faithful church's desired outcomes than any other means. Unbelievers need to hear the good news about Jesus, and they hear it best straight from the word of God. Those who want practical guidance for day-to-day life can find an abundance of it in the pages of Scripture. And those who think that the Bible is too simplistic to stimulate their minds really do have some amazing surprises in store for them when they start to plumb the immeasurable depths of God's revelation to us that fills its pages. The word of God is not inadequate or lacking for anyone in any circumstance. Rather, it is always full of rich blessings.

There is another form of preaching that is not completely devoid of a biblical basis, but it is still relatively thin in its use of Scripture. We call this "springboarding." A preacher starts with a biblical text, but really just uses it as a platform from which to dive into alternative, nonbiblical teaching. An example might be a preacher offering a sermon entitled "God Is Love" and starting by demonstrating that this truth can be found in 1 John 4:8. From here, though, he might fail to explain the significance of John's statement in its original context (where it is used to reinforce the fact that anyone who fails to love does not know God) or as part of the argument that John is unfolding in his whole letter, let alone as part of the overall message of the Bible, which centers on the death and resurrection of Jesus the Messiah. Instead, a springboarder might simply turn this statement into a headline under which he goes on to talk about his own experiences of love, to recite a great love poem, to share a touching love story, or something similar. We can learn a lot from other people's experiences and appreciate much in good poetry, and there may be a place for such things as helpful illustrations in a biblical sermon. But once they come to dominate the message and so marginalize the exposition of the Bible passage on which the sermon is ostensibly based, the preacher may well have failed his main purpose of faithfully teaching and applying the Scriptures.

Of course, many churches do regularly teach from the Bible, and there can be truly excellent Bible teaching in churches that are not attempting to teach the *whole* Bible. That has certainly been our most common experience in the churches we have either visited, belonged to, or served in. The pattern we have most frequently seen during the main weekly services includes a significant portion of time given to the ministry of the word, which tends to begin with the public reading of one or more Bible passages before the preacher explains and applies at least one of those texts to the congregation. It is important to be crystal clear at this point and say that we are completely in support of this practice—it is what we pray would happen every week in every church in every part of the world! But the point we are continuing to make is not about the biblical faithfulness of *individual sermons*, but about the place that those sermons have in an *overall preaching program* that is designed to communicate the whole counsel of God to a congregation over a given period of time. And so, just as we have been blessed by many, many great and faithful sermons in the churches we have been privileged to attend, it is also true that many of the great sermons we have heard have been stand-alone. By this we mean that a great sermon on, say, Romans 5 might have been followed by a great sermon on Galatians 5 the week after, while the week after that, the text being spoken from might have been Isaiah 60. Each of these sermons might have been most excellent in and of themselves, but they had no particular relationship to one another, and they were not part of a program seeking to systematically teach the whole Bible.

Of course, churches often do preach sermons in meaningful series such that the sermon on Romans 5 is followed by one on Romans 6, then Romans 7, and so on. This practice makes much more sense, as it helps regular attendees of the church learn more than just what Romans 5 has to say; over time, with a long enough series, it can help them learn what the book of Romans *as a whole* says, and how each chapter says what it says *in the context of the whole*. This is perhaps more important than we sometimes remember because God gave us the Scriptures as a collection of coherent works, not as a series of disjunct chapters or passages. Paul's letter to the Romans has a start, a middle, and an end, and Romans 5 has a very particular place in its flow. The individual chapters were not intended to be abstracted from the whole letter, and ultimately they have their full meaning only in the context of the whole letter.[1] There is a great Christian tradition of committing individual verses of Scripture to memory, and this is no bad thing. But there is a risk that comes with thinking about the Bible as just a collection of verses, and it is that we fail to read each verse in its right context. The same applies to Bible chapters taken out of their books. Preaching series that move linearly through whole books of the Bible reduce the risk of decontextualization or atomization of any part of those books. In addition, the practice of preaching in series also has enormous benefits for sermon preparation, something we will return to in chapter 7.

---

1. Our current chapterization of the Bible was normalized only in the medieval period, and versification was not standardized until the sixteenth century.

As good as it is to preach sermon series that progress through whole books of the Bible, even this is not enough because the problem we noted above with stand-alone sermons applies equally to stand-alone teaching series. That is, a church might have a series preaching through all of Romans, and then follow it with a series on, say, 1 Samuel, and then a series on Titus, but with no real rationale in place for determining which series will come when and how they together will combine to build up the church's overall teaching program. We know of a congregation where the usual practice was to preach coherent series of sermons from different books of the Bible, but upon looking into its history of preaching over almost a decade, we found that there had never been a single series from any of the Old Testament history books, only one from the Wisdom Literature, and just two from the non-Pauline New Testament letters. Moreover, many of the series were abbreviated, working through sections of longer books of the Bible, but never making it through those books from start to finish. As good as the sermons and sermon series were at this church, they were not part of a master plan that aimed to methodically work through the entire Bible, and a review of what the pastors had been preaching showed how patchwork their overall approach had been.

In addition to congregations missing out on learning from large parts of the Scriptures when no master preaching plan is in place, a church or preacher can end up putting some standard or favorite texts on high rotation. So it might be that over a ten-year period, a congregation not only misses out on hearing anything from the Writing Prophets, but hears three or four sermons on Mark 4:1–20. The people may not have any teaching from Leviticus, Numbers, or Deuteronomy, but get several series from Paul's letters. Given that Paul's letters account for around 5.5 percent of the Bible and those last three books of the Pentateuch take up about 8.9 percent, it is at least worth asking whether some churches have a bias that misrepresents the balance of what God has given us in his revelation.

Another thing that can happen without a master preaching plan is that churches can be excessively reactive in deciding what will be preached. They can focus on selecting texts or topics that address immediate situations. Of course, in many cases, this is precisely what a church must do. There would be a most unhelpful, and even unhealthy, disconnect from reality if major current world events, local happenings, or congregational situations were never appropriately engaged from the pulpit. This would only confirm some people's belief that the church's message is largely irrelevant.

But while there is always the need to demonstrate the direct relevance of God's word to prevailing circumstances, it is also important to let the Bible set our agenda and not just respond to events. There is a significant difference between going to the Bible with the question "What does God say about X?" and going to the Bible just asking, "What does God say?" In the first case, our minds are focused on a question or issue that we have decided we want to learn more about. In the second, we come open and ready to hear whatever God has to say, even if it ends up being about matters that we are not much thinking about beforehand. There is nothing wrong with the first approach; indeed, it is exactly right that we should seek the answers to our various questions from the Bible. But the power of the second approach is that it lets the Bible set the agenda and shape our whole outlook on life. We do not just look to the Bible to fill in the blanks or to add color to our predrawn outlines, but we look to it to paint the whole canvas of our worldview from scratch. This is actually a great gift to us, because the best way to live is in line with the patterns that God has determined for us. When we come to the Bible open to being shaped by its concerns, priorities, and agendas, we not only learn those patterns, but we may also be helped by having some of the issues that otherwise consume us put into their proper perspective. Our renewal as God's people happens when our minds are transformed not just by the absorption of new information, but by the right shaping and prioritizing of all that we know.

Sometimes churches work both to show the importance of the whole Bible and to capture its emphases by preaching "overview series" or "highlights packages." An overview series aims to summarize a large section of the Bible without focusing on any particular part of that section in detail. For example, an overview series might try to summarize all of Exodus 21–40 in three sermons, with the first explaining covenant laws, the second talking about the design and construction of the tabernacle and the setting aside of priests, and the third explaining the ongoing mercy of God toward a people who failed to live up to the Ten Commandments. Similarly, there could be a series on the early history of Israel in the promised land that offered one sermon on the events of the book of Judges, one on the lives of Samuel and Saul, and one on David and Solomon.

A highlights package is slightly different in that it does not seek to cover large swaths of the Bible quickly, but instead focuses on a series of short passages that are considered to be the most important in the large section. So an Exodus 21–40 three-sermon highlights package might start with one sermon that zeroes in on Exodus 31:1–11, where Bezalel and Oholiab are named as the craftsmen who will fashion the tabernacle, its furnishings, and the priestly garments. Its next sermon might then expound Exodus 32–33, where the Israelites make and worship the golden calf, and Moses intercedes to God for their forgiveness. The last sermon might then be on Exodus 40:34–38, where the glory of God fills the completed tabernacle. The highlights package of Israel's early history in the promised land might take its first sermon from Judges 15–16 to tell some of the story of the famous Samson as an example of one of the judges of Israel; its second from 1 Samuel 3 to introduce Samuel as a prophet; and its last from 1 Samuel 17, where the young David defeats the Philistine champion Goliath.

Both overview series and highlights packages have value; they can be very helpful in filling in the overall story of the Bible and helping congregations learn about some of the most significant moments—or at least those we have deemed to be the most significant. This is, of course, what most children's Bibles do as a way of familiarizing little ones with God's big picture. Ultimately, however, overview series and highlights packages alone are inadequate because their great benefit of showing so much so quickly is countered by their great weakness of passing over so much detail. They are a bit like watching a movie in fast-forward mode or just catching glances at it while walking in and out of a room. Some reasonable sense of it might be gained, but this is far removed from the fullness of what its creator wanted to convey.

Beyond this, there is another significant cost of teaching in overview series and highlights packages. It is that once they are done, a church is very unlikely to ever go back and look more closely at the detail that was skipped over because the leaders mistakenly believe that all the text has been adequately covered. How likely is a pastor to follow a three-sermon series on Exodus 21–40 with a fuller series that looks at all that is in those chapters in detail? The reality is that after a short summary series, the bulk of that text is unlikely to be revisited soon, if ever. And so, when thinking about the second half of Exodus, this means that no additional time might be given to learning more about restitution, sabbath, celebrations, the presence of God, the approach to God, the setting aside of leaders, daily worship, the manifestation of the glory of God, covenant renewal, freewill offerings, or any of the many other things that we learn from that part of the Bible—things that God had inscripturated for the good of his people. We should note here that preaching Exodus 21–40 well is unlikely to mean preaching one sermon for each of those chapters; the text itself might require a different approach (we will discuss this more in chap. 8). Our point is simply that the fullness of the texts should be preached, not skipped.

Finally, another two forms of preaching that are found in many faithful (but not whole-Bible) churches are what might be called "topical preaching" and "doctrinal-paradigm preaching."

In topical preaching, the preacher consciously seeks to cast biblical light on a particular subject or issue for the congregation. "Sex and Relationships" is perhaps one of the most popular topics that is addressed this way, although there are countless others: money, prayer, work, mission, science, faith, science and faith, terrorism, refugees, or whatever is trending in the news, just to give a few examples. When addressing one of these topics, the preacher might choose to exposit just one biblical text, such as Luke 21:1–4 for money, or might choose to survey a range of scriptural texts that all interact with the topic in order to present a more comprehensive biblical picture. Of course, these types of sermons can actually be incredibly helpful to listeners, especially if the topics addressed intersect with those that the Bible itself prioritizes.

Doctrinal-paradigm preaching differs from topical preaching in two ways. The first is that it always focuses on the one idea that the preacher believes controls the whole Bible storyline and teaching. For Protestants, this idea is commonly something like justification by faith. To be completely clear at this point, we are strongly of the view that justification by faith is an absolutely core and indispensable doctrine of the Christian faith, and that it does indeed run like a golden thread and supporting beam throughout the whole Bible. If you fail to understand and embrace it, you have really failed to understand and embrace something at the very center of Christian belief. Having said that, though, we are also of the view that justification by faith is not the sole or main point of every single passage of Scripture. Therefore, if a preacher ends up expounding the doctrine of justification by faith in every single sermon, irrespective of which text he is preaching from, there is a good chance that he is actually more committed to preaching his doctrinal paradigm than the message of the text before him. It is very important for us to be balanced in making this point. We do believe that there can be, must be, and are controlling ideas that prevent us from focusing on minor or esoteric points in the texts we are preaching, and again, an overarching understanding of the priority and means of justification is a critical part of this. But at the same time, we want to say that preaching that insists on always and only outlining the same doctrinal paradigm over and over will never deliver the fullness of what the Bible teaches.

There is another way that doctrinal-paradigm sermons differ from topical sermons, and it is that they often go undetected. While a talk entitled "Sex and Relationships" is obviously topical, sermons entitled "Jews and Gentiles," "2 Peter 3," or "Modern Atheism" might all actually end up being doctrinal-paradigm sermons in disguise. This is because some preachers are so deeply convicted about their overarching doctrinal position that they either consciously or subconsciously end up making it the main point of everything they teach. In the Jew-Gentile sermon, the main point becomes that both must realize they are justified by faith. Similarly, though 2 Peter 3 points to the coming day of judgment for those who scoff at the long-suffering hope of Christian believers, the main point of this sermon can become that scoffers need to turn to Christ and so be justified by faith. And the sermon on atheism explains that they are trying to create an acceptable godless morality, but what they really need is to be justified by faith.

Once again, it is essential that we make our point well here. We are absolutely *not* saying that justification by faith is a less-than-primary part of the Bible's message. In fact, we would probably include it in our own teaching on Jews and Gentiles, 2 Peter 3, and modern atheism in some of the ways summarized above. All we want to say at this stage is that this controlling paradigm, or any other, may not adequately exhaust the fullness of what God wants us to know about given texts or topics. If we are to faithfully preach every part of the Bible, we must do so in a way that captures the *unique emphases of every part*, and even when we rightly bring our doctrinal paradigm to a passage, we must not stamp it over the top of the text in a way that makes the particular focus of the passage practically irrelevant. To put it another way, we could say that there is a difference between preaching the text doctrinally or theologically and using the text as a vehicle for preaching our doctrine or theology. The former is essential, but the latter, at worst, puts us at risk of not really preaching the text at all.

Having thought about what it might look like to work from a preaching program that does not attempt to preach the whole Bible, we will now turn to thinking about some of the impacts of such a failure.

## Consequences of Not Preaching the Whole Bible

If there are a variety of ways that preachers can teach less than the whole Bible, it is worth considering what effects that could have. Ultimately, the common outcome is that congregation members hear less than the whole counsel of God, and the following are just some potential outworkings of this.

First, churchgoers who are not taught the whole Bible might end up with a practical belief that there is a "canon within the canon." As *canon* is the term used to refer to the collection of writings that are together understood to comprise holy Scripture, so "canon within the canon" is used to indicate a portion of the Bible that is considered to be more important—perhaps more important *to God*—than the rest, with the obvious implication being that the rest is less important and therefore optional *for us*. Of course, few Christians would explicitly suggest or subscribe to such an idea. But if, for example, a pastor were committed to preaching one third of his sermons from Paul's letters and never preached anything from the Old Testament prophets, it would not be surprising to find that members of his church came to subconsciously think that Paul's writings are essential for Christian life and faith, but that there is nothing of critical importance to be gained from reading Obadiah or Habakkuk. There are two related issues here. One is the lack of formation that church members might have as a consequence of their imbalanced diet of Scripture, and the other is a low practical view of the Bible as a whole.

A second and connected problem of not preaching the whole Bible is that congregation members might end up with a narrow or imbalanced theology. If we believe that God has something useful to say to us in every part of Scripture and that it is not all repetition of the same point (even though there certainly is some purposeful repetition; see chap. 8), then we must conclude that majoring on some parts of Scripture at the expense of others may have the effect of amplifying some of the things that God is communicating to us while dampening others. There is absolutely nothing wrong with wanting to turn up the volume on what God has to say to his world through various parts of the Bible—unless a result of doing so is that we mute the volume elsewhere. This is like having a canon within the canon, but at the level of our doctrine. We might say it is having a core theology within our full theology.

Again, we must be careful to be balanced as we outline this risk. It may well be right that we have a core theology or controlling doctrinal paradigm. Sometimes churches refer to things in this category as "matters of first importance" or "gospel issues," and it is, in fact, necessary to make this distinction, as we will discuss in part 2 below. But the risk is that we can focus so much on the core theology or gospel issues that we ignore other matters that may indeed be secondary, but which are not therefore altogether unimportant. Unfortunately, humans can sometimes really struggle with recognizing that some things are truly good when we know other things are even better. Instead, we can tend to rightly acknowledge what is best, but then clumsily contrast everything else against it as being either bad or relatively worthless. This is a terrible mistake when it comes to our theology because, while the gospel may truly be the most important thing, there are yet many other very, very important things that God reveals to us in his word, and we cannot justify giving them scant attention on the grounds that they are only secondary matters. They are still secondary matters revealed by the God of the universe himself for the benefit of his people.

One of the most serious manifestations of an imbalanced theology is a narrow gospel, and unfortunately, even some of the great Bible-believing and Bible-teaching churches have at times failed to teach the full gospel to their people because they have focused their preaching around those parts of the Bible that highlight one aspect of the gospel rather than another. The best example of this in recent generations is the lack of emphasis on Jesus's resurrection in many Western churches. While it is abundantly clear in the Bible that the gospel of Jesus includes the message of his resurrection, some preachers seem to communicate that the gospel message is focused on the cross alone, as though Good Friday is the sole heart of the Christian story, with Easter Sunday just being something of a curtain call. The cross is indeed absolutely central to the Christian message, as countless biblical texts plainly show. But preaching from these texts alone could have the effect of building a gospel theology that does not include resurrection and eschatology in any meaningful way, and which is therefore dangerously imbalanced.

A final consequence of not preaching the whole Bible is that members of the church might never grasp the overall message and shape of the Scriptures. To continue using an example we have already presented, if a preacher gave a disproportionate amount of time to teaching Paul's letters, the church might be impoverished in its understanding of the great metanarrative of the Old Testament. The people of that congregation might learn a great deal from Paul's understanding of the work of Christ and how his followers should live together, but they could miss out on seeing how Christ came as the climax of the story of Israel. It could even be that from Paul they might learn lots of propositional truths, or Bible bullet points, but not the unfolding history of God's work that is recorded throughout the Bible. Like the other consequences, the bottom line is that if the whole Bible is not preached, the people of God might only learn a trimmed-down version of all that God has for them in his word.

We want more than that for the church and the world, and so we will now explicitly lay out the core challenge of this book.

# The Challenge

So far in this book, we have presented our fundamental beliefs about the whole Bible as the word of God, and we have considered the various ways that even Bible-believing preachers do not deliver the whole counsel of God to their congregations, along with some of the implications of that. To some extent, all of this has been preparatory for the core challenge that we now want to put forward. Our challenge is this:

> All vocational preachers should set themselves the goal of preaching through the entire Bible over a thirty-five-year period.

By this, we mean preaching through every biblical book from start to finish as a coherent whole. And that means every chapter of every book, and every verse of every chapter—the whole lot! The thirty-five-year period is a little arbitrary, but it is an attempt to approximate a solid lifetime of preaching in a concrete number; a time frame that is significantly long, but not vague and open-ended. Of course, as outrageous as this challenge might sound, it is really little more than calling preachers to convert their basic beliefs about the Bible into a practical commitment. We actually believe that the challenge issues itself: as preachers, if we really believe our doctrine of Scripture, what else can we do?

As you digest this goal, you might be having one of a number of reactions. Perhaps you feel very excited because you love the idea of putting hard targets on big goals, as that helps you to imagine really achieving them. If you are this kind of person, your mind might be buzzing with excitement and racing forward as you think about what this will look like for the years of preaching that you have before you. However, we recognize that perhaps you are not this type of person and are feeling something quite different. You might be feeling drained and exhausted at just the thought of taking on such a monumental task, especially if you are already working hard in pastoral ministry and feel that adding even small projects into the calendar is difficult. Perhaps you are feeling dismissive because you think the idea of preaching through the whole Bible is such a ridiculous pipe dream that it seems like a waste of time to even consider it.

We are very conscious of the personal and practical realities, and the unpredictable events, of pastoral ministry that make this challenge all the more difficult. Both of us have served as preachers in churches for years. But we still think working toward preaching the whole Bible is not only ideal, but also realistic. One thing that might help the task seem a little more approachable is just remembering that if you have a weekly preaching ministry, you are going to be preaching regularly anyway, and so whether or not you take on this challenge, you are still going to be doing a considerable amount of work preparing sermons over the years. Indeed, we are not suggesting that you need to preach any *more* sermons than you otherwise would, just that you should plan your preaching programs in such a way that you can aim to cover the full text of Scripture over the course of your preaching career. Also, much of the rest of this book is geared toward addressing the practicalities and human considerations, both individual and corporate, that are implicit in our challenge. We believe this approach to the ministry of the word has benefits for all who take it up or experience it.

So let us now move into part 2, where we address the many questions that add up to the big "how" question: How can we preach the entire Bible? The chapters that follow will engage many practical matters, but we need to start by considering theology and the theological frameworks that must be in place as we preach through all the different parts of Scripture.

# PART 2

# HOW TO PREACH
# THE WHOLE BIBLE

4

# Understanding the Whole Bible Theologically

It is not by accident that the Bible is a big book—over one thousand pages of relatively small print in most English translations. This is because our God has generously supplied us with a great deal to know about himself, his work, ourselves, the people around us, and the wider world. All of that revelation simply would not fit into a smaller book. Moreover, as we have already seen, within its many pages, the Bible also contains different types of writings by different authors who wrote to different people at different times, and who addressed different issues and different situations.

But this variety does not mean that all of the parts of the Bible are largely unrelated to one another, as though in the Bible God has given us a great, but somewhat random, collection of things that he wants us to know about. The Bible is not like a dictionary or encyclopedia. People can safely open those kinds of reference books (or search those kinds of websites) to read single entries without needing to worry at all about things such as metanarratives, binding themes, harmony with other entries, and so on because such works are not designed with much concern for those things. The detail of each part can be profitably studied without any need to consider the rest. However, the Bible is not like that. It is not only a big and diverse book, it is also a *complex and unified* book in which all of the parts are meaningfully related to all others in many ways. The Bible is like a detailed tapestry with many threads that weave in and around many others to make up both tiny images and big patterns. No thread makes sense of everything on its own. And no thread makes complete sense in relation to just one or two others. But each contributes to a vast interrelated whole, and that whole gives the reason for the color, place, and direction of each individual thread.

In a similar way, as much as we are committed to giving our full attention to every unique part of the Bible, we can never ignore the whole as we do so. At the most obvious level, if we were to preach sermons, or sermon series, without showing the proper connections to the other parts of the Bible, we would send the message that there are parts of Scripture that are not meaningfully connected to the rest—threads that are not part of any tapestry. But the problem with this kind of preaching runs far deeper, right down to the level of our interpretation. If we fail to recognize the holistic nature of the whole Bible as we expound any one part, we are also likely to misunderstand that part, because none of the parts makes full sense in isolation from the whole.

Before moving on to more practical advice, we want to use this chapter and the next to consider the most important tools we have for understanding and communicating every part of the Scriptures in ways that respect and reflect the unity of the Bible as a whole. Those tools are our theologies and theological frameworks.

## What Is "Theology" and Why Does It Matter?

Just what is "theology"? One of the standard responses to this question, and a good place to start, is to think about the origin of the word itself. Technically, the word *theology* comes from the Greek words *theos* (θεός), meaning "God," and *logos* (λόγος). While *logos* literally means "word"—that is, a communication—it can also be used to refer to the underlying reflection to which that word gives expression. So *theology* can therefore mean thinking and reasoning about God. Given this basic and broad definition, we are able to accept that there can be not only much different content to theology, depending on *what* people think about God, but also many different types of theology, depending on *how* people think about God, or on how different groups of people approach the task of thinking about God and then organize their conclusions in various ways.

Having a conscious theology, or theological framework, helps us bring a common mind to each part of Scripture and to interpret it consistently. For example, if we understand the maxim "God is love" to be the touchstone of all right belief about God—if "God is love" is at the core of our theology—we will approach every part of Scripture on the assumption that it somehow gives expression to this core idea. This is easy to see when we consider the parable of the prodigal son from Luke 15:11–32, but it is harder to find in passages such as 1 Kings 18:39–40, where Elijah instructs those who have just declared "The LORD, he is God" to seize the prophets of Baal so that they might be slaughtered. Having such a theology is helpful to us because it means we will be thinking about each part of the Bible through a common and unifying lens, but it is also risky in that it might lead us to find things in our texts that are only secondarily present, such as God's love in the 1 Kings 18 example. It is also potentially not just risky, but actually quite dangerous, if our theology is wrong. That is, if we bring a flawed understanding of God and his ways to our preaching texts and then read those mistakes into those passages, we could end up preaching sermons that distort the Bible and, at worst, even proclaim heresy. Obviously we must do all we can to avoid anything approaching this.

Although necessarily circular, the best way to avoid imposing bad theology on the Bible is to draw our theology from the Bible in the first place. Earlier, we spoke about our approach to preaching being shaped by the fact that all Scripture is God-breathed—that is, inspired by him. If this is correct, and Scripture is the only infallible guide to knowledge about God and the things of God, it naturally follows that there is no better place to establish our theology. Over the rest of this chapter, we will present three theological frameworks—ways of thinking about theology—that are grounded in the Bible, as well as some of the basic content of theology in each framework. It is necessary to have all three, as there is no single, simple theological grid that can serve us if we want to understand the whole Bible correctly, far less a pithy aphorism such as "God is love." Even if that is a most profound and deep truth, it is not enough of an interpretive guide to help us understand every part of the Bible in its own integrity. The three frameworks below each have strengths and weaknesses, but together they give us a helpful grid for considering each passage of Scripture in light of the truths and shape of the rest.

Before outlining the frameworks, we need to clarify a potential confusion that arises from the nomenclature we are using. Although one of our theological frameworks is called "biblical theology," it will become apparent upon reading our descriptions of the other two that they are equally biblical in the sense that they draw their content from the Bible. The difference in the three frameworks is not in the source of their assertions, but in how they organize theological thought.

## Biblical Theology

Biblical theology is part of the discipline of interpreting a passage. However, where exegesis seeks to understand and interpret all the mechanisms that an author has used in communicating the message that he wants the reader to hear, biblical theology seeks to understand what the author is communicating *theologically* and how that fits into the larger theology of the Bible that finds its focus, center, and goal in Jesus Christ. From its start to its end, the Bible tells a grand story, and every passage of Scripture is located somewhere within that story. To understand a passage we must first know where it fits. This much is straightforward enough, but the particular work of biblical theology is not only to locate a passage *chronologically*, but—as its name suggests— to locate it *theologically*. The goal is to understand the theology of the passage itself; where that theology fits into the progress of the revelation of God's purposes outlined in the Bible, which find their focus in Jesus; how it engages with the theological priorities of the Bible already revealed; and how it contributes to further develop that theological revelation. It requires us to "read below the surface of the text" to see how each passage of narrative, poem, letter, or other part of Scripture is engaging with the big theological story.

So biblical theology enables us to read the story of David and Goliath and see that it is more than a story of God's side winning and his opponents losing in a military confrontation. Rather, it is a story of God's people needing salvation and of God raising up an unexpected deliverer who would represent the whole nation and later become their great shepherd-king (2 Sam. 5:2). When the story of David's victory is recast this way, we understand it in terms of the Bible's big story, and we recognize its resonances with the Bible's major theological themes and movements. Using biblical theology, we can quickly see far more than the chronological place of David's story in the history of God's people. The surface story interacts with a bigger plotline, but the theological story interacts with the major thematic and theological movements of the metanarrative. The surface story is immediately obvious, but the theological story needs to be discerned by theological awareness.

In the same way that the structure of biblical theology follows Scripture's metanarrative, its content is also characteristically divided into categories that are drawn from the story. This is in contrast to systematic theology (which we will consider next), which often devises synthetic categories, such as "hamartiology," "Christology," and "pneumatology."

So what is the overarching theological plotline of the Bible that binds and shapes each part? And what are the major moments and developments that are thematically determinative of the whole story?

Naturally, it is instructive to examine the beginning and end of the canon of Scripture for orientation to its overarching narrative. At the very start of the Bible, we observe that God creates the world (Gen. 1:1–2:3) and that the pinnacle of his creative activity is human beings (1:26–28). In addition, we see that human beings are integral to God's purposes for his creation, and that humanity and the creation as a whole are directed toward a goal: rest in him (2:1–3). Once his work of creation is complete, God says that all he has made is "very good" (1:31), indicating that, at this point, the creation is fit for its intended purpose and can move toward its goal without hindrance.

We could represent all of this diagrammatically in the following manner.

Fig. 4.1. Scripture as a Text with a Direction.

The first chapters of Genesis unfortunately also demonstrate that God's good intentions for his creation are corrupted by humans as they act in independence and rebellion. Hence, by the end of chapter 3 we find that rebellious humanity has rejected God, fallen short of his ideal, and consequently been shut out of his presence. This leaves men and women off course and heading for eternal disaster, now only able to hope against hope that there might be some solution that will still allow for restoration and for God's ideals to be met (which is hinted at in the Lord's words to Eve in Gen. 3:15).

From this big-picture setup of Genesis 1–3, we can turn to the other end of the Bible's story to find out how things will end up. Revelation 22:1–5 describes an Eden-like garden with a river and bountiful trees; the end of Scripture is clearly meant to evoke thoughts of the beginning and images of how that beginning was developed in Scripture (e.g., from a garden to a garden-city, the new Jerusalem). But now the situation is good once more. Humans can live in the new creation; the tree of life, from which they were barred in Genesis 3, is accessible again; and God himself is with his people (Rev. 21:2). This is a place where there is no barrier between humanity and God, and therefore, what we have at the end of the Bible is an assurance of restoration, resolution of the problems of Genesis 3, and fulfillment of God's purposes. The question is, How? What is the turn in the Bible's plotline that leads to this good conclusion?

Of course, the answer, easily found throughout the New Testament, is Jesus. He is also here in the last chapters of Revelation, presented as the Lamb, as he has been a great many times in this last book of the Bible since 5:1–6. There we see that the Lamb is the only one who can unfold divine history, represented as a great scroll with seals that need to be removed (vv. 1–5). We also see that he rises from Israel's royal tribe of Judah and the line of the great King David, and that he holds a place higher than all other creatures at the very throne of God (vv. 5–6). Finally, we see that he is "standing, as though [he] had been slain" (v. 6). The last phrase is strange; it is hard to imagine exactly how someone would stand if he had been slain. But the image makes immediate sense when we know it is pointing back to the culminating acts of Jesus's ministry—his very real death and miraculous resurrection to new life. Seeing this slain-but-risen Lamb center stage at the end of the Bible story makes it clear that he is the one who brings us from the disaster of Genesis 3 to the renewed and eternal garden city of Revelation 21–22. He is at the center of God's largest purposes, and he makes them possible. We could represent this final picture with another diagram.

Fig. 4.2. The Turning Point of the Narrative of Scripture.

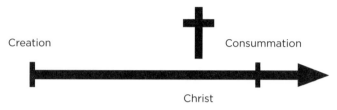

Even with only this simplest construction of biblical theology drawn from the beginning and end of the Christian canon, we can see that the Bible's storyline, and its theology, are centered on God's work in the person of Jesus Christ. This means that a good understanding of any part of the Bible recognizes this core, just as our consideration of the David and Goliath story did. As it engages the themes of deliverance from disaster and establishment of a great king, we see it pointing us quite directly to Jesus. In some cases, a passage's interaction with the major theological movements of the biblical metanarrative is not so obvious, but the fact that the Bible is a unified work assures us that it is there. As we read within the light of God's critical and key work done in Christ, we read and understand the Bible as God intends.

## Systematic Theology

Given that biblical theology directs us to think about how any part of Scripture intersects with the major theological movements of the whole, how does systematic theology differ?

Before answering, it is again critical to remember that good systematic theology is no less biblical than biblical theology. That is, although its approach and purpose are different, systematic theology is equally focused on understanding the teaching of the Bible. This is an especially important point to make given that systematic theology as a discipline has often been criticized for being too abstract and pointless. To be fair, these criticisms have sometimes been justified. The famous question "How many angels can dance on the head of a pin?" is commonly put forward as a mocking example of the kind of issues that systematic theologians are thought to spend their time puzzling over. The truth is, while that particular question is not asked by any serious systematicians, there are plenty of other explorations that do seem equally useless.

Part of the problem is that historically there has been a blurring of theology and philosophy, with the result that some systematicians have ended up giving time to what might be better described as "philosophical theology," which does give attention to the angels-on-a-pinhead speculations that are a long way removed from anything that the Bible seems to be concerned with. There are some legitimately important questions that can be asked by philosophical theology, but it is helpful to recognize that they are not the questions of systematic theology proper. In addition to not being the same as philosophical theology, neither is systematic theology the same thing as historical theology, the latter being the study of the writings of significant biblical scholars over the ages. It is without doubt true that we can benefit enormously from studying the thoughts of the great ones. However, our primary goal is not to become experts in, say, what Augustine believed about grace, but rather to understand what the Bible says about grace. As we aim to work that out, we might well read Augustine at length, but we do so only to see what light his thoughts throw on the Bible, not just so that we can understand them for their own sake.

True systematic theology, then, is really nothing more than an attempt to synthesize the whole Bible's teaching on the subjects and themes that it addresses. This work is done in recognition that the Scriptures are not shaped like a theological dictionary and so do not present decontextualized information ordered under topic headings, but also that there are times when it can be very helpful to have biblical teaching laid out this way—including when we are preparing sermons. Having quick access to a balanced summary of what the Bible teaches on topics such as grace, pride, or even Jesus will serve us well when we come to preach on texts where those topics are in view, as it will enable us to consider the words of our particular passages evenhandedly, conscious of what other parts of the Bible say that might temper, nuance, or thicken up our understanding of the texts before us.

Of course, anyone who reads the Bible knows that we could draw hundreds, or even thousands, of topics from across its pages, meaning that even if good systematic theology deals only with biblical matters, it could still be esoteric and overdone. We could ask, What does the Bible say about serving in the military, leisure time, dating, education, fine art, politics, eating candy, wearing long trousers, or any number of other topics? In some cases, the Bible offers us quite a lot of information, and it can be a real blessing to the church to have balanced input on matters that we all know are immediately relevant to our daily lives.

But systematic theology does more than just answer those "What does the Bible say about . . . ?" questions. It also helps us think well about the priority of, and the relationships between, the various subjects engaged by the Scriptures.

Thinking about priority, we can imagine that, at some point, we may need to scour the Bible for all that it teaches on sex. Clearly this is a subject on which we all need a balanced biblical understanding (especially in the West, where sexual norms are being rapidly and radically redefined). As we do that work, though, we need to recognize that sex is not, in fact, one of the most primary things that the Bible teaches us about. To be sure, we can learn a great deal about sex from books such as Genesis, Song of Solomon, 1 Corinthians, and several others, but good and full as this teaching is, we would never be able to conclude that the Bible is a book about sex. As we think about the emphases and movements of the whole Bible (things that our biblical theology helps us focus on), we see that topics such as God's gracious nature and works, human sinfulness, Jesus's death on the cross, and the coming judgment are of far more concern to the biblical writers. This is why these kinds of topics tend to form the major headings in systematic theology textbooks, whereas sex does not. Good systematic theology therefore not only gives us syntheses of those matters that the Bible addresses, it also helps restrain us from majoring on the minors or making mountains out of molehills.

We can go even further with systematic theology and see that in addition to giving us a comprehensive and balanced view on a given topic, and a sense of the priority of that topic in the Bible as a whole, it also locates our understanding of a given topic within the full web of biblical teaching. Take the example of alcohol consumption. If we are thinking systematically, we quickly see that this is not a primary matter in the Bible, but that there are many things for us to learn. We also see that the question of drinking alcohol interacts with many of the Bible's truly big topics. We see that alcohol is a good part of God's creation, that it can be terribly abused through human sinfulness, that wine regularly symbolizes the sacrifice of Christ for the forgiveness of our sins, and that it will be well used in the new creation as believers share in the great banquet with Jesus. Creation, sin, forgiveness, and new creation are all major biblical themes and therefore major headings of systematic theology (as well as biblical theology). Therefore, our understanding of alcohol consumption should be strongly informed both by texts that directly address it and by our understanding of each of these major areas of theology. And, of course, our understanding also must be set within the broader relationships between those major areas.

It is worth noting in passing that one of the most important parts of any systematic theology textbook is its table of contents. This is not only because it tells us which pages we need to turn to in order to read about different topics, but because there we see the structure of the author's theological framework laid out. We see what the author thinks the major areas of theology are, and where secondary and tertiary matters fit beneath them. This helps us know which controlling theological themes we should have in mind when considering the various issues and topics that arise in the passages we preach.

To be good preachers of the whole Bible, we need to not only understand each biblical text in light of the progressive revelation of the Bible as a whole, but also to understand the topics touched on in each text in light of what the whole Bible says about them, with the appropriate weighting given to them and in right relationship to the Bible's major emphases. We therefore need to have a good working framework of systematic theology, and also to be able to do our own systematic theology. Many preachers gain their systematic framework from the courses they take during their years in seminary. If you have not had that experience, it might be well worth seeing if there are opportunities to take such classes as part of your ongoing development as a preacher. If you are not able to do that, at the very least it would be worth getting one of the standard systematic theology textbooks, reading through it, and then keeping it handy for reference. While there are many good systematic theology texts, unfortunately none of them is perfect and all have certain biases. This means judicious reading is always important.[1]

## Gospel Theology

Unlike biblical theology and systematic theology, "gospel theology" is not a widely used term and does not refer to a generally accepted approach to studying the Bible. Rather, it is a framework for thinking that we want to promote here because we believe it is very helpful for pastors and teachers who want to work at preaching the whole Bible. Technically, gospel theology can be understood as a version of systematic theology that sees the gospel

---

1. One recent volume with deep historical understanding, clear structure, and accessible style is Gerald Bray, *God Is Love: A Biblical and Systematic Theology* (Wheaton, IL: Crossway, 2012). A larger work worth consulting is Herman Bavinck, *Reformed Dogmatics*, 4 vols. (Grand Rapids, MI: Baker Academic, 2003–2008).

of Jesus as the single biggest topic in the Bible and as the message that brings coherence to every part of the Bible. That is to say, we believe that everything God has revealed to us in the Bible fits into an overarching gospel schema, whether it has to do with creation, sin, Jesus, grace, sex, alcohol, or anything else. This is quite a grand claim, and its validity, of course, partly depends on how we define the gospel.

Unsurprisingly, we believe that the best way to define the gospel is the way the Bible does, and that the clear and consistent teaching of the Bible is that the gospel is the message about Jesus the Messiah, who died and rose again. This is what we find explicitly stated in texts such as 1 Corinthians 15:3–5, which says that the gospel is "that Christ died for our sins in accordance with the Scriptures, that he was buried, that he was raised on the third day in accordance with the Scriptures, and that he appeared [to Peter and numerous other people]." Similarly, 2 Timothy 2:8 directly states the gospel as "Jesus Christ, risen from the dead," before also stating that Jesus was "the offspring of David" to underscore his messianic credentials. These explicit summaries of the gospel crystallize what is fleshed out all through the New Testament in many ways: God's good news is that Jesus is the King who died for his people and rose again to new and eternal life.

As straightforward as this is, in order to think about the gospel theologically, we must go further than simply stating facts and also work to understand the meaning of those facts. What does it mean that Jesus is King, that he died, and that he rose again?

In theological terms, the gospel divides into three categories: Christology (concerning Jesus the King), atonement (concerning his death and its implications for humanity), and eschatology (concerning his resurrection and its implications for the future of the creation, as well as ethics). It is our view that these three big gospel themes are the macrocategories into which all of the Bible's teaching can be fit. So, for example, when the Bible teaches us about God, its primary way of doing so is through Jesus, the King of God's kingdom, who makes his Father known (e.g., John 1:18; Col. 1:15; Heb. 1:3). When the Bible teaches us about ourselves as humanity and as individual people before God, it is very clear that our greatest need is for the salvation from sin and death that Jesus brings (e.g., Matt. 1:21; Rom. 5:8). And when the Bible shows us that the risen Jesus is the "firstfruits" of the new creation, into which his people will follow him (e.g., 1 Cor. 15:20–22), it brings hope and certainty about eternity. The gospel categories guide us into right thinking about all of the major concerns of the Bible.

But what then of other things that the Bible teaches? Again, we believe they too fall under these categories. Here are a few random examples. The Bible's teaching on priesthood finds its fulfillment in the person and work of Jesus (e.g., Hebrews 7), which is the focus of Christology. The many strong things that the Bible says about judgment have to do with human rebellion and sin, which require divine atonement. What the Bible says about marriage prefigures the eschatological relationship between Christ and his church (e.g., Eph. 5:21–33; Rev. 21:1–4). When the New Testament teaches on morality, it is calling us to live now the type of life that we will live in our resurrected eternity (e.g., Col. 3:1–4). And when we learn about evangelism in the Scriptures, we are driven to declare Jesus as Lord (Christology), to call people to repent of their sins and to trust the effectiveness of Jesus's death for them (atonement), and to proclaim the hope and joy of eternal life (eschatology). We could continue, but the point should be clear enough.

This chapter has sought to outline three types of theology— biblical, systematic, and gospel—and to show their importance for well-balanced and well-integrated reading of the whole Bible and of each individual part of it. In the next chapter, we will move on to consider how we can use these theologies to help us faithfully preach each part of the Bible to our congregations.

However, before we move on, it is worth noting explicitly something that has been implicit throughout this chapter—that the divide between the three types of theology is somewhat artificial. We have already stated that good systematic theology is deeply biblical and that gospel theology is a type of systematic theology. It should also be clear that the emphases of gospel theology significantly overlap with those of biblical theology. This means that in practice, we do not need to mechanically look at each passage of Scripture through each of the three separate theological lenses in turn. Rather, we want to approach each text through a holistic, integrated theological grid that appreciates the thematic movements of the developing Bible story, understands the breadth, balance, and relationships of the subjects being addressed, and recognizes the priority of the message of the crucified and risen Lord Jesus everywhere. Over time and with practice, understanding the Bible this way becomes more and more natural and intuitive. For our current purposes, however, it will be helpful to continue distinguishing our three types of theology in their own right as we consider how each helps us preach the whole of the Bible.

5

# Preaching the Whole Bible Theologically

In the previous chapter, we discussed three biblically grounded approaches to theology that can help us understand each part of Scripture in sympathy, harmony, and balance with the rest, and in recognition of the fact that the whole canon has a deep unity. Far from being an abstract academic discipline that is a step removed from straightforward Bible reading, our theology profoundly controls the ways we interpret each part of Scripture. Although not everyone articulates his or her theological framework, everyone has one, even if it operates only at the subconscious level. None of us is neutral; we all bring a set of beliefs and presuppositions to our reading of the Bible. Given this, it makes sense for us to think about our theology and to develop our theological thinking in ways that will help us interpret each passage of Scripture well.

In this chapter, we want to build on the last and start to consider how our theological thinking not only affects our interpretation of the Scriptures, but also how that interpretation can play out as we begin to shape sermons. We will consider these questions for each of our three theologies.

## Using Biblical Theology in Preaching

In the world we live in, our challenge in preaching the whole counsel of God is exacerbated by two factors. The first is that fewer and fewer people have a grasp of the Bible's overarching storyline, and many are altogether unaware that the Bible even has such a storyline. Two generations ago, the majority of children in the West were raised learning not only basic Bible stories, but also something of the thread of the narrative that binds them all together. It began in Eden, went on to Noah and his ark, and then came to Moses, the parting of the Red Sea, and the Ten Commandments. There was the establishment of the Israelite nation, and the role of prophets, priests, and kings. Jesus was born to Mary, and he was kind, radical, and powerful in lots of ways. He died on the cross, rose again, went to heaven, and is going to come back and make all things perfect in the end. Of course, if we die before then, we will go to heaven too if we trust in him. As thin as this is, it is a basic structure upon which teaching from across the whole Bible can be built. But for many today, even this much is lacking.

The second factor that makes preaching the Bible more difficult today is that people are losing the ability to find underlying meaning in the texts they read. While most readers can recount the plot of the novel they have been reading, a surprisingly small number under the age of forty can explain much of the author's purpose in writing the novel, or the themes that are being explored. They read at a surface level only. What are the Harry Potter books about? Easy—a boy wizard growing up as the hero the world needs. But why did J. K. Rowling write this story, and what themes does it explore? There are good answers to these questions, but it is not so easy for even some avid fans to articulate those answers. Our generation does not always think about texts this way, and this sets people back a long way when it comes to understanding the parts of a very long book like the Bible. This means that it is critical for us to foreground biblical theology in our preaching. We must constantly orient our hearers to the larger story and its theology as we preach it in small sections, and we must always be showing them the resonances between the parts and the whole. In doing this, we not only explain the passages more fully, we also build up their understanding of the Bible's metanarrative, its major theological emphases and developments.

We can illustrate what it looks like to preach using the perspective of biblical theology by imagining a sermon on Ezekiel 11:1–25, where the Spirit foretells judgment upon wicked counselors and restoration for the people of Israel. Without any biblical theological framework, we might think of preaching this sermon at just the surface level: God will indeed judge those who are wicked, but his people will be given new hearts and a secure place with him. This is all true, but it is quite generic (it is the sort of application you could draw from hundreds of texts) and decontextualized—that is, it misses some key parts of the text and their connections to the greater story of God and his people that is told over the span of the whole Bible. But if we notice that the whole chapter is set in "the house of the Lord" (v. 1) and in the time of Israel's exile (vv. 15–16), we can immediately begin to see some deeper significances to the events that are reported in this chapter.

The "house" refers to the Jerusalem temple, which lay at the geographic and spiritual center of the land of Israel, and was where God was known to specially manifest his presence among his people (1 Kings 8:1–11). The exile was the time of God's judgment on his old covenant people for rejecting his ways after they settled in the promised land. Here, then, we see God proclaiming judgment on those who had the central responsibility for leading his people in his good ways, but who instead led them into sin. We also see that the people who were scattered would be brought back home and established in right ways once more. This all means that even in the midst of their deserved exile out of the presence of God, the people of Israel had a real hope for restoration. This has distant echoes of the arc from Genesis 3, where the first people were exiled from the garden of Eden, to Revelation 21–22, where humanity is restored to right and joyful living in the presence of God.

Ezekiel 11 therefore teaches us not just something general about God being on the side of the righteous and opposed to the wicked, or just something very specific about the predicted course of ancient Israel's history. It also stands as an anticipation of the final solution that God will bring for his people's universal predicament, and it thus both cleaves into and highlights the macrostory of the Bible, which was as important to the exiled Israelites as it is to us. If we explain these things as we preach this text, we are able to bring it as a living word to our congregations. We can show them, from the beginning of the Bible and right through the Old Testament, that God's ways are constant, his purposes are on track, and even if we are suffering in the midst of our own sinfulness, we are not without hope. The passage also points squarely to Jesus himself, who similarly looks upon the temple and pronounces judgment (Mark 13:1–2), and who is presented as the replacement for the temple as the locus of worship for God's people (John 2:13–21). Moreover, in John 16:7–11, Jesus teaches us that he is the one who will send the heart-changing Spirit predicted in Ezekiel 11:19. Ezekiel 11 is not an esoteric text; rather, it is woven into the central story of the whole Bible, and it needs to be understood and preached with that in view.

As another example of biblical theology getting us to the right meaning of a text, we can look at Hebrews 1:1–2:9. This is a particularly instructive passage, as the author of Hebrews himself seems to employ biblical theology here. The epistle begins with a magnificent exaltation of God's Son. Through the Son, the Father has spoken more clearly and definitively than ever before (1:1–2). The Son is the maker and inheritor of all things (1:2). The Son bears the Father's image, and his work is thorough and completed (1:3). He is superior even over the angels (1:4–14), and the message about him must be adhered to (2:1–4). In this context, the writer turns his attention to Psalm 8, which itself is a theological reflection on Genesis 1:26–27. Suddenly the focus is off Jesus and on human beings, who received rule from God but failed to rule as they ought (Heb. 2:7–8), a recap of what we already know from Genesis 3. However, verse 9 then shows how the Son is the key to the story and the solution to the problem. It tells us that the Son, named now as Jesus, was the particular human who came from above the angels to fulfill the mandate given to Adam. He faced the suffering of death so that his people would not have to, and is now crowned with glory and honor. In the New Testament, the writer of Hebrews is looking back to retell the story of Jesus, who is the climax of the story of the Old Testament. Biblical theology comes right to the surface in this passage.

In both of these examples, we see that biblical theology helps our preaching both by locating our texts in the biblical storyline and, more importantly, also finding the connections of each passage to the big theological movements of Scripture. If we bring a biblical theological approach to our preaching, Jesus will always be at the center.

## Using Systematic Theology in Preaching

Perhaps the best known work of systematic theology ever written is John Calvin's *Institutes of the Christian Religion*. Despite now being more than 450 years old, this work remains the enduring benchmark of Reformed theology, and many of today's theologians regularly draw from the *Institutes* in their ongoing work. As famous as the *Institutes* is, though, Calvin's purpose in writing it has not always been noted. The following quotation is from an extended statement entitled "Subject of the Present Work" that Calvin included with the prefatory materials of the *Institutes*, and it is very instructive as to the relationship between systematic theology and Bible reading:

> Although the holy Scriptures contain a perfect doctrine, to which nothing can be added—our Lord having been pleased

therein to unfold the infinite treasures of his wisdom—still every person not intimately acquainted with them, stands in need of some guidance and direction, as to what he ought to look for in them, that he may not wander up and down, but pursue a certain path, and so attain the end to which the Holy Spirit invites him. . . .

I dare not to bear too strong a testimony in its [the *Institutes*'] favor, and declare how profitable the reading of it will be, lest I should seem to prize my own work too highly. However, I may promise this much, that it will be a kind of key opening up to all the children of God a right and ready access to the understanding of the sacred volume [the Bible]. Wherefore, should our Lord give me henceforth means and opportunity of composing some commentaries, I will use the greatest possible brevity, as there will be no occasion to make long digressions, seeing that I have in a manner deduced at length all the articles which pertain to Christianity. . . .

I exhort all who reverence the word of the Lord, to read it [the *Institutes*], and diligently imprint it on their memory, if they would, in the first place, have a summary of Christian doctrine, and, in the second place, an introduction to the profitable reading both of the Old and New Testament.[1]

From what he has written here, we see that Calvin viewed his systematic theology as a *servant* of good Bible reading. Rather than being purely concerned that people know theological arguments or bullet points of doctrine, Calvin saw that knowing the Bible as it is written is the highest goal. This is perhaps the opposite of what we might sometimes intuitively think—that the point of Bible reading is to gather enough data to formulate systematic positions on theological matters. While there is nothing wrong with this, Calvin shows us that right understanding is as much about soaking in and following the Scriptures well as it is about

---

1. John Calvin, *Institutes of the Christian Religion*, trans. Henry Beveridge, 2 vols. (London: James Clarke & Co., Limited, 1962), 1:22–23.

extracting truths from them. Of course, the process is circular, as the more we read the Bible, the more we refine our systematic understanding of the topics it teaches us about, and then, in turn, that refined understanding helps us read the Bible better. Nonetheless, as far as Calvin was concerned, good Bible reading was the goal and systematic theology was the aid.

His commitment to good Bible reading is evidenced in the fact that while the *Institutes* may well be his magnum opus, he penned far more words as he fulfilled his goal of composing commentaries—he wrote them for over half of the books of the Bible. And although quite extensive as a collection, Calvin's commentaries are far briefer than they would have been had he not also produced the *Institutes*, because, as he noted, he did not need "to make long digressions" in the commentaries in order to explain every theological question that was raised by the texts, but could assume his readers approached his expositions through the grid of his systematic work.

In addition to less distracted Bible reading, the other benefit Calvin anticipated coming from the *Institutes* was that those who had them in mind would be able to "pursue a certain path" through the Scriptures and "not wander up and down." That is to say, he felt that having a systematic theology in place would allow every passage of Scripture to be read in light of a broader, balanced theological understanding. This is absolutely critical for preventing the misinterpretations that might arise when any one text is used in isolation to arrive at theological conclusions.

For example, if we were to draw conclusions about the work of the Holy Spirit by reading Acts 2:1–4 alone, we might surmise that we should always expect the Spirit's coming to be attended by rushing wind, the appearance of hovering, divided tongues of fire, and the ability for believers to speak foreign languages. This would be problematic, as few people have ever had this experience, so if this understanding were preached to a congregation, many could reasonably conclude that the Spirit had never come to them. That would be quite disturbing for Christian believers! But of course Acts 2:1–4 is not the fullness of what the Bible teaches about the work of the Spirit in believers' lives. Indeed, 1 Corinthians 12:4–11 explicitly states that "there are varieties of gifts, but the same Spirit" (v. 4) and "To each is given the manifestation of the Spirit for the common good" (v. 7). With even just these extra truths about the work of the Spirit in mind, we could prepare a sermon on Acts 2 in a more correct and helpful way as being a particular manifestation of the Spirit at a particular time for the common good. Furthermore, if we were to do a more comprehensive systematic theology of the Holy Spirit, we would see that the "common good" that the Spirit enables has to do with helping people follow Jesus. And in Acts 2, this was exactly the good that was done for a large group. Verses 5–11 go on to tell us how:

> Now there were dwelling in Jerusalem Jews, devout men from every nation under heaven. And at this sound the multitude came together, and they were bewildered, because each one was hearing them speak in his own language . . . "[about] the mighty works of God."

The particular manifestation of the Spirit at Pentecost enabled many people to hear, in their own languages, what God had been doing. The apostle Peter then elaborated the gospel (showing how it was in accordance with the Old Testament Scriptures) and called the crowd to repent and be baptized in response, with the promise that they too would receive the Holy Spirit. Amazingly, around three thousand people were baptized that day, and while they would have received the Spirit as Peter said, it is noteworthy for us that there is no mention at this point of any rushing wind or fiery tongues. The manifestation of the Spirit may have been different from what it was in another part of even the same chapter of the Bible. So we see that our systematic theology—as well as our contextualized reading of the passage—makes a huge difference to the lessons we take away from the text about the work of the Holy Spirit. The same conclusion could be illustrated with respect to any number of other theological beliefs and any number of passages of Scripture.

It is a relatively small step to translate what we have seen about the importance of systematic theology for Bible reading to its importance for preaching. If the preacher is the primary interpreter of the Scriptures for a congregation of God's people and those with whom they are seeking to share the faith, then his reading of the Bible shapes the reading of many other people. One reader narrowly interpreting the work of the Holy Spirit after having read just one passage without a systematic theological framework is a problem. But if a preacher were to deliver that narrow understanding from the platform, the problem would be multiplied by the number of people who accepted it—which, in an obedient church, could be a lot! The preacher's job is to teach and apply the text correctly, and he needs systematic theology to do this.

He especially needs it if he is planning to preach through the whole Bible, because, as he does that, he will have to teach many, many passages of Scripture that, on their own, could be significantly misinterpreted. What might be misunderstood if someone preached Colossians 1, which describes Jesus as "the firstborn of all creation" (v. 15), without an underlying systematic picture of him that accounts for such texts as John 10:30, where he says, "I and the Father are one"? What if a preacher exhorted a congregation in his sermon on Romans 12 to "live peaceably with all" (v. 18) without offering any nuance that might be brought from a fuller theology that incorporates texts such as Matthew 10:22, where Jesus teaches that "you will be hated by all for my name's sake"? And what might be wrongly assumed from a sermon on Matthew 1 that highlighted the arrival of Jesus as "God with us" (v. 23) without factoring in the truth captured in Psalm 139:7–10, which asserts that no one has ever been able to flee from God's presence? In all cases, the lack of a well-developed systematic theological framework could lead to a preacher overemphasizing one biblical truth in such a way as to diminish others, distorting the overall revelation of God. Preachers who do not preach all of the Bible but just a smaller subset of "key" Bible texts find this less of a problem, as they feel freer to pick and choose passages that do not require a judicious theological mind to get right, but that simply make the points they want to make. However, they will, of course, create many of the other problems that come with not preaching the whole counsel of God, such as those we discussed in chapter 2.

Hopefully we have made it clear that *using* systematic theology in preaching is not the same thing as *preaching* systematic theology. It is not a discipline that invites us to do things such as using Acts 2:1–4 as a springboard for outlining a comprehensive biblical picture of the Holy Spirit. Rather, its purpose is to provide a balanced understanding of the teachings of the Bible that allow us to make carefully judged statements when preaching any text and prevent us from overplaying or narrowing an idea in ways that give an imbalanced or distorted picture of the whole counsel of God. Again, systematic theology never occupies a higher place than the text of the Bible itself. Calvin's words from the close of his "Subject of the Present Work" hit the right note: "Above all things, I would recommend that recourse be had to Scripture in considering the proofs which I adduce from it."[2]

## Using Gospel Theology in Preaching

Part of the beauty of the gospel message is that it is simultaneously straightforward enough that most anyone can grasp it (with the Spirit's help), but too deep and profound for anyone to ever truly exhaust its fullness. The identity of Jesus is simple at one level, but completely incomprehensible at another. The atonement can likewise be clearly explained in a couple of sentences, but is also the subject of great tomes that have been written to try to flesh out the entirety of its meaning, without any having managed to fully

---

2. Calvin, *Institutes of the Christian Religion*, 1:23.

succeed. Similarly, the resurrection can make immediate sense to a small child, but still leave philosophers perplexed. This is all very exciting because it means that the gospel is neither elusive nor tedious; there is always more about it that we can search out, but we never need worry that we might miss it altogether as we do so. If our contention from chapter 4 is correct, and every part of the Bible is governed by and contributes to the theology of the gospel in some way, then preaching through the whole Bible is nothing less than helping people learn more of the fullness of the good news of Jesus. Every sermon from across the whole canon of Scripture should throw more light on the message of Jesus, his death and resurrection. Every sermon can and should be a gospel sermon.[3]

As we think about gospel sermons, it is very important that we remember that it is a mistake to think that the gospel is useful only for unbelievers, and that those who are Christian believers do not need to hear it anymore, as though it is old news and therefore no longer important for them. It is very sadly true that this sort of understanding exists in some churches today. Even some churches that would never explicitly say such a thing can show that it is what they believe through their practice. Perhaps this is most obviously seen when churches have special evangelistic services, for which they prime their members by letting them know that the sermons will be particularly clear presentations of the gospel, and so will provide a great opportunity for them to invite unbelieving friends to hear the news of salvation and hope. As great as this is, if we have a pervasive gospel theology, we find ourselves hearing about the special evangelistic sermons and asking, "Isn't the gospel clearly presented in *every* sermon?" The idea that we could have some "gospel" sermons and some "non-gospel" sermons would suggest an understanding of the Bible that does not recognize the gospel as being expressed in different ways throughout the whole.

3. See Timothy Keller, *Center Church: Doing Balanced, Gospel-Centered Ministry in Your City* (Grand Rapids, MI: Zondervan, 2012), 77–79.

It would be too much to say that there should never be especially evangelistic sermons, because it is true enough that in some parts of the Bible, the call of the gospel is more obvious, explicit, or related to the cultural moment than in other parts. But even so, there are some questions worth exploring here. Can God use only some parts of his word to reveal himself to unbelievers? Should believers ever expect "low-gospel" sermons to be part of what they hear in their regular church services? Are gospel-focused sermons especially important only for unbelievers? (The fact that some believers choose not to go to church on weeks when there are special evangelistic sermons might betray that, at some level, this is what they believe.) For now, it is enough to press the point that because we believe the gospel is present everywhere in the Bible, every sermon should have gospel content.

What exactly does a sermon preached with due attention to gospel theology look like? Probably the simplest way to explain is by considering some brief examples. If a preacher were preaching through 2 Chronicles, what would he make of chapter 21, with its account of Jehoram, the terrible king of Judah? There is much of great importance to learn from this story about what leaders most definitely should not do—such as killing their brothers and others who might have a claim on power, or leading God's people into unfaithful practices. These sorts of things attract the judgment of the Lord and can lead to personal as well as national ruin. The story also reminds us of the incredible mercy and faithfulness of God, who, despite the sins of Jehoram, did not destroy the house of David because of his commitment to the covenant he had made (v. 7). But as right, good, and helpful as all this is, there are also great gospel connections that can be more explicitly made throughout this chapter. One is that God's people ultimately have only one true and worthy king, Jesus Christ himself. Unlike Jehoram, Jesus was the Father's perfect representative, as the fullness of God was pleased to dwell in him (Col. 1:19). He therefore did not lead the people astray, but showed them the right way to worship the Father (e.g., John 4:21–26). And rather than killing his brothers for fear that they might steal his power, Jesus set out to redeem us so that we might be adopted into God's family and become coheirs with him (Gal. 4:4–7). He is the kind of king that Jehoram makes us long for: a king in the line of David, but even better than David. This text really leads us to remember the identity of Jesus, one of the core parts of our gospel theology.

What if a preacher were expounding Esther 6:14–7:10, where the final downfall of Haman, the highest official of King Ahasuerus and the great enemy of the Jews, is recounted? Aside from being part of a riveting story, there are many great lessons in this passage for a preacher to develop. Here Esther, after having already shown incredible courage in chapter 5 by seeking an audience with the king—who could take her life for doing so (4:11)—unfolds her plan for winning more of the king's favor through her extended banquet. Having done this, she then petitions him not to have the Jews (including herself) killed according to Haman's plan. At this point, Ahasuerus sides with Esther, whom he has seen only as good, so the lives of the Jews are secured.

No doubt there are many ways in which a preacher could demonstrate that good character and strategic, patient actions like Esther's can be used to achieve great ends for God's people. But this chapter is also striking for the way it illustrates God's flawless justice. In the end, the megalomaniacal Haman is hanged on the very gallows that he had set up for Esther's relative Mordecai, the one who first ignited Haman's hatred of the Jews. Thus, the evil of Haman's heart and actions is dealt with perfectly; he gets precisely no more and no less than he deserves. The scales of justice sit completely balanced at the end of his story. When we reflect on God's perfect justice, our gospel theology drives us back to Christ's cross and the atonement that he made there. If God's justice requires a reckoning for every single wrongdoing, then sooner or later, our wrongdoings need to meet that justice. By rights, we should pay the fair price for our own sin, just the way that Haman paid for his. But rather than us being hoisted up a gallows for all of our sins, the gospel says that Jesus was hoisted up on a cross in our place. Against the stark backdrop of Haman's fate, we are overwhelmed by the deep love of Jesus, who substituted for us. Even in Esther, the one book of the Bible that does not explicitly mention God, his gospel message still shines through.

As a final example, how would a sermon on 1 Thessalonians 4:1–8, with its focus on sexual purity, communicate the gospel? Of course, a preacher would want to be very straightforward in outlining the moral imperative of this text to his congregation. In the first instance, the plain directive to avoid fornication must be unambiguously highlighted, especially in light of the very serious consequences that Paul spells out for his readers. Any preachers who fail to pass on these plain warnings of Scripture to the people they minister to fail to represent God. But as important as this is, it is also necessary to ensure that the moral teaching of this text is healthily anchored in the gospel. Sometimes preachers fail to make this type of connection, and the people who hear their sermons can be left wondering how the message of grace in Christ relates to the necessity of living certain ways as his followers. The first thing to say is that both are absolutely true, and there can be no room whatsoever for the idea that Christ's atoning death means that our behavior does not matter. On the contrary, it is precisely because our behavior matters so much that we needed Jesus to die for us. Of course the message of grace remains, and when preaching a passage such as 1 Thessalonians 4:1–8, it is always important to remind the congregation that if they know they have failed in the past to live up to what the text calls for, they can always turn to Christ for forgiveness. That does not mean that their misconduct was not so bad after all or that there will never be other actions they might need to take in order to set things right with those against whom they have sinned. But it does mean that divine forgiveness is always on offer for those who come in penitence and faith to the Savior.

Once we have ensured that this assurance is included in the sermon, we can look beyond the ways that the gospel addresses our historic behaviors to how it affects our future living. The key in this passage is the notion of the spiritual transformation of believers. In 1 Thessalonians 4:3, Paul says that our sexual purity is part of our "sanctification" or "holiness," and the idea of believers being holy is repeated again in verses 4 and 7. Then, in verse 8, Paul explains that a rejection of this teaching is a rejection of "God, who gives his Holy Spirit to you." The idea is that God's people are able to live holy lives because they have the Holy Spirit within them. The connection to gospel theology is that the Spirit is the pledge or "guarantee of our inheritance until we acquire possession of it" (Eph. 1:14). This is eschatological language that looks forward to us receiving all that we have been promised in Christ. In terms of our physicality, that means our resurrection bodies will be fully Spirit-animated and completely free from sinfulness when Jesus returns (1 Cor. 15:35–57). This, in turn, means that the gospel imperative lying behind the call to be sexually pure is really just a call to be who we will be in eternity when we are resurrected like Jesus—indeed, who we really are already as Spirit-indwelled believers. With our gospel theology framework, we in no way dilute the moral imperative of the text, but we do see it as part of the big and eternal work of transformation that God is doing in his people.

———

Over the past two chapters we have outlined three overlapping types of Bible-based theology that we believe work together to give us a faithful approach to preparing a sermon on a passage of Scripture. With this theology in place, we can be confident to preach the whole Bible to our people without fear that the "obscure" texts will not tie in with the "core" texts, and with excitement as we realize that a full diet of Scripture gives people a deep exposure to the gospel.

From here we will move into more practical advice that will help us preach the whole counsel of God, and we will start by thinking about planning our preaching programs.

6

# Big-Picture Planning

The core conviction of this book is that it is essential for the people of God to hear as much of the Bible preached as possible. It therefore follows that preachers need to plan their preaching well by developing thoughtful long-range preaching programs.

Some preachers who love the Bible and always preach sermons from it still do not think much about which texts they are going to preach week by week. While their priority is on biblical preaching, they do not give much time to *planning* their biblical preaching. Others tend to think of their preaching in series, and as a result, they do plan for packages of maybe six to ten sermons at a time, which is helpful over the course of a couple of months, but not beyond that. Then there are some preachers who plan multiple preaching series, and so always have a sense for what they will be preaching several months ahead.

However, as encouraging as this is, it is rare to find preachers who go much further and think about the balance of biblical teaching that they will bring to their congregations over the course of several years, let alone decades or even a lifetime. Many preachers do not think this far ahead partly because it can be hard to see the value in so much planning; they know that they will preach something from the Bible and instinctively feel that whatever particular texts they choose will be adequate to keep the congregation faithful. Therefore, rather than spend time scheduling in the sermon texts that they will preach the April after next, they focus their energy on the very real and more immediate pressures of ongoing, daily Christian ministry. And even if they can see the theoretical value in longer-range planning, they may reason that because there are always unknowns around every corner in congregational life, there is little point to planning for a time when they have no idea at all what might be on their plates.

As much as we understand these reasons that preachers do not plan their preaching, we would argue that there is far, far more to be gained than lost in prioritizing long-term planning of a preaching program. As we have already argued, preachers should be aiming for more than just biblical sermons that maintain a solid baseline of faithfulness. They should be doing all they can to broaden and deepen their people through the fullest diet of Scripture possible.

In this chapter, we will discuss some of the top conceptual commitments that need to be made before we even begin planning our preaching programs. In the next chapter, we will offer some very practical suggestions for filling out the specific details of a working preaching schedule.

## Good Planning Takes Good Time

The first step in effective planning is the step of planning to plan.[1] That is, we need to commit to setting aside good time to do the work of planning our sermon series for the months and years ahead, and even the work of sketching out our longer-term preaching goals. For many preachers, this may be something that they have never thought of doing. It is certainly not something that is much taught in most seminaries, where the focus rarely

---

1. This idea is taken from Peter Brain, *Going the Distance: How to Stay Fit for a Lifetime of Ministry* (Kingsford, Australia: Matthias Media, 2004), 174–75.

goes beyond preparing individual sermons. But the leader of a church must also take responsibility for designing and building the church's whole teaching program, not just delivering stand-alone sermons.

For many of us who are preachers, it may be a good discipline to set aside something like a week or even half a week each year just to plan our preaching programs. Perhaps this could even be a time when we get out of our normal routines altogether so we can really focus on this critical high-level work. A few days away from the office, or at least with regular meetings cancelled and regular lines of communication closed, can make a significant difference to doing good, deep work rather than just quickly cobbling something together without properly thinking and praying through it all. It is always hard to carve out this time, because there is never a shortage of work to do in pastoral ministry, but we would argue that if pastoral ministry is grounded in good ministry of the word, planning this ministry deserves time and attention. Just because it is possible to get by without doing this does not mean that is acceptable or good in the long run. It may also be possible to get by in Christian ministry without visiting church members or without much prayer. But that does not mean either of these practices is faithful or healthy. We give time to the things we value, and if we preachers value our people and the whole Bible, we ought to give time to preparing a balanced diet.

Beyond the level of our basic responsibilities, we also believe that good planning has the potential to make each sermon better, simply because it gives us lots more brooding or "stewing" time. If we know in the backs of our minds that we will be preaching through Malachi two Aprils from now, then our ears are likely to prick up when we hear someone speaking about the Minor Prophets; we are likely to tune in a little more and perhaps even jot a few quick notes. Similarly, if we happen to come across a good blog post on Malachi while we are looking online for something else, we will know to bookmark it or save it to a folder we have set up for our Malachi sermon materials so that it is there when we come to do our preparation. If we are in a Christian bookstore and happen to see a good commentary on Malachi that is on sale, we might take the opportunity to buy it at the cheaper price, knowing that we will need to get it at some point anyway. If we are at a missions conference and hear that one of the presenters will be giving some reflections from Malachi, we might choose that session over another to see if there are helpful things to be learned in it. Over the course of a couple of years, all of our fortuitous accumulations can actually add up to quite a good collection of materials, information, and thinking that we will be very thankful for when we get into preparing our Malachi series. No doubt, our congregations will be thankful for the deeper sermons too.

## Offering a Balanced Diet of Scripture

Once we have made the in-principle decision to attempt to preach the entire Bible over thirty-five years and the practical commitment to plan our preaching well, the first thing we need to think about is what will make up a balanced diet of Scripture in our context. We need to consider how much we plan to preach to our people from each Testament, corpus, and genre, and over what time period we will offer them the balance.

One simple approach could be to preach through the Bible just as it is laid out, from Genesis to Revelation. The great benefit of this approach would be that it would respect and follow the Bible's own metanarrative and structure. And it does make considerable sense to preach through the books of the Bible in the order they are arranged in most English Bibles, because many of them progressively build on each other. Deuteronomy presupposes a familiarity with Numbers. The book of 2 Kings presupposes a familiarity with 1 Kings. The Gospels presuppose a familiarity with the Old Testament. Revelation presupposes a familiarity with all of the biblical books that come before it.

However, many parts of the Bible are in parallel rather than in sequence with other parts (think of the relationship of 1 Samuel–2 Kings to 1 and 2 Chronicles, and the relationship of the four Gospels to one another) or are arranged using a different system altogether (think of Paul's letters, which are normally arranged from longest to shortest).

In addition, even though the idea of preaching through the Bible from front to back makes some sense at one level, the huge time frame we are considering would mean that the benefit of it would probably be lost. It might be incredibly helpful for individuals to move through the whole Bible from cover to cover in a single year of their daily devotional readings, but one sermon per week over thirty-five years is a different dynamic. We think that it is probably not ideal for one of Jesus's churches to spend twenty-five years in the Old Testament before it ever gets to hear any exposition from one of the primary accounts of their Lord and Savior's life, death, and resurrection. Even with great biblical, systematic, and gospel theologies, we feel this approach would be unhelpfully imbalanced.

One common way that preachers conceptualize their preaching programs is to aim for one-quarter Old Testament, one-quarter Gospels, one-quarter other New Testament writings, and one-quarter topical sermons over the course of a year. At a first glance, this also appears to be a reasonable way of offering a varied diet of Scripture, but there are a few problems inherent in it. One is that there is considerably more New Testament than Old Testament in this plan, despite the fact that the Old Testament is much longer than the New. In fact, if we imagine this program being populated with weekly preaching texts of roughly equal length (something that we actually think is a very bad idea, as we will explain in chaps. 7 and 8), then we would run out of New Testament relatively quickly, in perhaps five to ten years, while having preached maybe less than a quarter of the Old. In addition, a paradigm like this does not help much when it comes to finer detailed planning for preaching through all of the different parts of the Old Testament in a balanced way. For example, it would be quite possible to be faithful to this paradigm and to go for ten years without ever preaching much from the Prophets or Writings. In order to even out the long-term balance some more, we need to answer two important questions: "What are the right subgroupings of Scripture to preach?" and "What is the time period over which we are looking for balance?"

We have used the language of "diet" already a few times, and perhaps developing that image a little more at this point will help us think about how we can wisely carve up our preaching plans. We know that our food is meaningfully divided into five groups—carbohydrates, fruits and vegetables, dairy, proteins, and fats—and that we need to eat a good balance of these to be healthy. Over the course of a day, we know we need various amounts of each of the food groups, but we might not balance them all at every meal. Our breakfast might have lots of carbohydrates and dairy, but not so much vegetables or proteins. But then we might get our vegetables in a salad at lunch. And we might have proteins, vegetables, and fats in our evening meal, but not as much carbohydrates. No single meal gets the daily balance right, but together they do. Recognizing this gives us freedom to change things from time to time; we might decide one day to have a high-protein breakfast and a high-carbohydrate lunch, but then a vegetarian meal in the evening. Things might be rearranged, but the tallies at the end of the day can be the same.

We could also helpfully broaden our thinking to our diet over the course of a whole week. In this case, it might be that if we know we have a special meal coming up one evening where there will be a lot of proteins and fats, we can plan to counterbalance this imbalance by having a little less fat the days before and after so that our overall weekly intake is the same as a normal week.

Finally, we can think about our long-term eating plans and habits, which have to do not with particular meals or particular weeks but with our ongoing patterns, making sure that we are not eating junk food very often, that we regularly have plenty of fresh fruits and vegetables, that we incorporate whole grains into our cooking, that we are sparing with salt and sugar, and so on.[2]

For many of us, all of this is simply common sense, and so it should be easy for us to transfer the same sort of thinking to our preaching—something we should especially want to do given that feeding people a good diet of Scripture is even more important than feeding them healthy food.

The first thing to decide, then, is what are the main "food groups" that we need to keep in balance. Are they necessarily Old Testament, Gospels, other New Testament, and topical, or are there other possibilities?

## Divisions of the Canon

In chapter 2, we saw that beyond the division of the Bible into two Testaments, we can also recognize that the Old Testament is made up of three sections: Law, Prophets, and Writings. In Hebrew, these Scriptures are called the Tanak, which is an acronym of *Torah*, *Neviim*, and *Ketuvim*, the Hebrew names of the three parts. There are, in fact, many ways of further subdividing and grouping the books in both the Old and New Testaments. It is worth being conscious of these not only so that we understand what is being discussed when we see the terminology but, more importantly, because the ways we choose to group the books of the Bible will have some impact on how we decide to populate our preaching programs. The table on pages 126–127 shows some of the common subcategorizations of the biblical books.

---

2. Please note that we make no claims at all to be nutritionists and are using food here only as an everyday illustration. For good eating advice, you should read diet books written by recognized health-care professionals—not a book on preaching!

Fig. 6.1. Categories of Biblical Books.

## Old Testament

| BOOK | SEPTUAGINT DIVISIONS | HEBREW DIVISIONS | AUTHORS | GENRE |
|---|---|---|---|---|
| Genesis | | | | Narrative |
| Exodus | | | | |
| Leviticus | Law/Torah/Pentateuch | | Moses | |
| Numbers | | | | Narrative & Legal |
| Deuteronomy | | | | |
| Joshua | | Former Prophets | | Narrative |
| Judges | | | | |
| Ruth | | Writings | | |
| 1 Samuel | | | | |
| 2 Samuel | | Former Prophets | | |
| 1 Kings | History | | | |
| 2 Kings | | | | |
| 1 Chronicles | | | | |
| 2 Chronicles | | | Chronicler | |
| Ezra | | | | |
| Nehemiah | | Writings | | |
| Esther | | | | |
| Job | | | | Poetry |
| Psalms | | | David and Others | |
| Proverbs | Wisdom Literature | | | |
| Ecclesiastes | | | Solomon | |
| Song of Solomon | | | | Poetry |
| Isaiah | Preexilic Prophets | Latter/Major Prophets | | Prophecy |
| Jeremiah | | | Writing/Literary Prophets | |
| Lamentations | | Writings | | Poetry |
| Ezekiel | Exilic Prophet | Latter/Major Prophets | | Prophecy & Apocalyptic |
| Daniel | | Writings | | Narrative & Apocalyptic |
| Hosea | Preexilic Prophets | | | Prophecy |
| Joel | Postexilic Prophets | | | Prophecy & Apocalyptic |
| Amos | Preexilic Prophets | | | |
| Obadiah | Postexilic Prophets | | | |
| Jonah | | | | |
| Micah | | Latter/Minor Prophets/ Book of the Twelve | Writing/Literary Prophets | |
| Nahum | Preexilic Prophets | | | Prophecy |
| Habakkuk | | | | |
| Zephaniah | | | | |
| Haggai | | | | |
| Zechariah | Postexilic Prophets | | | |
| Malachi | | | | |

## New Testament

| BOOK | STANDARD DIVISIONS | | AUTHORS | GENRE |
|---|---|---|---|---|
| Matthew | Gospels | | Matthew | Narrative |
| Mark | | | Peter? | |
| Luke | | | Luke | |
| John | | | John | |
| Acts | | | Luke | |
| Romans | Pauline Epistles | | Paul | Epistle |
| 1 Corinthians | | | | |
| 2 Corinthians | | | | |
| Galatians | | | | |
| Ephesians | | | | |
| Philippians | | Prison Epistles | | |
| Colossians | | | | |
| 1 Thessalonians | | | | |
| 2 Thessalonians | | | | |
| 1 Timothy | | Pastoral Epistles | | |
| 2 Timothy | | | | |
| Titus | | | | |
| Philemon | | Prison Epistles | | |
| Hebrews | | | Uncertain | |
| James | | Catholic Epistles | James | |
| 1 Peter | Petrine Epistles | | Peter | |
| 2 Peter | | | | |
| 1 John | Johannine Epistles | | John | |
| 2 John | | | | |
| 3 John | | | | |
| Jude | | | Jude | |
| Revelation | | | John | Apocalyptic |

The way that many of these categories have been determined is obvious. The postexilic prophets are those who spoke to the people of God in the times after the exile in Babylon. The Johannine corpus is made up of those books commonly considered to have been written by the apostle John. The apocalyptic books are those that are apocalyptic in style and subject matter, and so on. There are, however, a few categories that may not be immediately self-explanatory. The distinction between "Former" and "Latter" Prophets, or "Former" and "Writing" Prophets, is that the Former Prophets are those books of the Old Testament that include accounts of the prophets of the earlier times of Israel, such as Samuel and Elijah, whereas the Latter or Writing Prophets are those books that were addressed to Israel at a later point in its history and that are not primarily made up of only historical narrative, but also capture the written messages and visions of those prophets.

Other groupings that may not be commonly known are the "Prison Epistles," which are those letters written by the apostle Paul when he was imprisoned; the "Pastoral Epistles," which are the three letters that Paul wrote to two individuals, Timothy and Titus, and that contain a great deal of instruction regarding the leadership of the church; and the "Catholic Epistles," which are those New Testament letters that have long been thought to have been addressed to a "catholic" or universal audience rather than to a specific local church. As is plain from the table above, many of the categories overlap, and—because there are no strict conventions among Christians as to how to refer to subgroupings of the Bible—this means that it is not uncommon to hear shifts from one set of language to another when discussing a book of the Bible by its category. So, for example, a conversation about the book of Ecclesiastes might refer to it as part of the Old Testament Writings, the Wisdom Literature, or the Solomonic corpus, all of which are true. To make matters even more complicated, some books of the Bible have a mixed content. For example, Ezekiel has sections of the narratival, prophetic, and apocalyptic genres, and Isaiah has pre- and postexilic sections, making these a little harder to fix into single rigid categories. Then there are books with disputed provenance, such as Joel, which is hard to tie confidently to a particular period of history.

Another important category distinction that is not included in the table above is that between what can be thought of as the foundational parts of each Testament and the remaining texts that draw on them. The difference highlighted here is not between those books of the Bible that are more doctrinally foundational and those that are not; that would cut against the central argument of this book. Rather, it is the recognition that some parts of the Bible are chronologically and literarily foundational, and others then continually build upon and point back to those foundations. In the Old Testament, the Law of Moses is foundational, with the Prophets and Writings continually building on and pointing the people back to those foundations in a range of different ways at different times in different circumstances. In the New Testament, the Gospels are foundational, with the book of Acts, the letters, and Revelation again pointing people back to the foundational records of Jesus in a range of ways.

Fig. 6.2. The Bible's Foundational Sections.

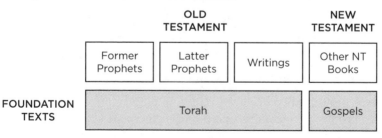

Once again, the main reason for being aware of all of these categories and categorizations is not to be constrained or controlled (or overwhelmed) by them, but simply to gain an appreciation of the natural affinities of the parts of the Scriptures, and then to be able to think about how those parts should be balanced against one another in a long-term preaching program. Only when we have done that will we be able to move on to filling in our preaching program with the particular texts that we will preach on particular days.

## Setting a Guiding Paradigm

Unfortunately, we cannot present the indisputably right or best paradigm with which to shape a multiyear preaching program, as many local factors need to be taken into account. What is ideal for one context may not be for another, and all paradigms have shortcomings that may be more or less problematic in different settings. What we will consider now is just one possibility that will allow us to demonstrate how an undergirding paradigm for a preaching program can be conceived and then practically implemented. Our hope is that this discussion will get us into the right headspace for the work of identifying our own convictions about preaching in our own contexts. As we go through this process, we will highlight some of the shortcomings of the paradigm we are offering here, again to show that there are no fully neat and tidy approaches to our task that we can implement without the need for careful, ongoing, and contextualized thought.

We have chosen to build our preaching program around a six-fold division of the Bible that largely reflects the historical shaping of the canon. In the Old Testament, we start by taking the Law, Prophets, and Writings as meaningful and distinct parts, but then also separate the Prophets into the Former Prophets and the Latter Prophets, both in recognition that these are different types of texts and also because the separation results in four approximately equally sized divisions. We then add the New Testament, divided in two parts that are also of roughly equal length, as has been common over the history of the church. The foundational part is the Gospels, and the remainder is made up of those documents of the early church that all assume some familiarity with the central teaching of the Gospels (even though some of this material pre-dates the formalization of the Gospel texts).

Having established these divisions, we might decide that we want to give each of them a share of our preaching program that is proportional to their length in the Bible. This would give us a paradigm in which we preach the biblical texts in the proportions shown in the chart below.

Fig. 6.3. The Bible in Six Divisions (Proportionally Weighted).

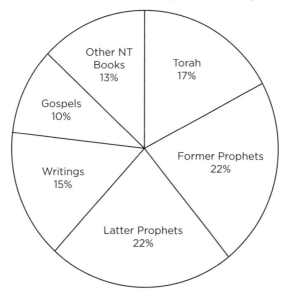

If we were to translate this paradigm to the number of sermons preached over the course of a fifty-two-week year, we might have nine sermons from the Law, twelve from the Former Prophets, twelve from the Latter Prophets, eight from the Writings, five from the Gospels, and six from the remainder of the New Testament. The nice thing about a program that allocates the number of sermons in proportion to the length of each part of the Scriptures like this is that it does not result in us running out of one part of the Bible before others, because we are teaching from across the parts of Scripture and not giving preference to a particular part.

But as we anticipated, there are real problems too. One is that we might decide that the climactic importance of the Gospels means that they need more than five of our sermons per year. We could decide to preach more from the Gospels, but of course we would then need to cut down on the preaching from another part of the Bible, perhaps one of the Old Testament sections, which could have implications years down the track when we need to increase the number of sermons from that other part of the Bible to keep pace with our progress through the Gospels.

However, it could be that we anticipate the length of our preaching texts from the Old Testament will be significantly longer than our New Testament passages, meaning that we will not run out of Gospels before we get through the Old Testament. That is to say that we suspect we will need more sermons per page of Scripture to cover the New Testament than the Old anyway. Following this thought, one way we could tweak our paradigm would be to normalize the number of sermons by the number of different sections of the Bible that we are working with. That would mean we would aim to preach eight or nine of our year's sermons on each of our six sections, as shown in our modified chart. This gives us more New Testament than before, but still reflects the Bible itself by having more Old Testament.

While we might feel that this breakdown gives us a better overall balance, there are still issues to address. For example, eight or nine sermons might not be the right amount for preaching a particular part of the Bible. If we decided to preach Job from the Writings, we would not be able to get through it all in nine sermons. And if we chose to preach Haggai as our text from the Latter Prophets, we might find it artificial to stretch it out over eight weeks. This raises the significant issues of maintaining each text's structural integrity while working it into our preaching calendars, breaking big biblical books down into smaller sections, and preaching our sermons in coherent series. All of these issues will be tackled in the next two chapters.

Fig. 6.4. The Bible in Six Divisions (Equally Weighted).

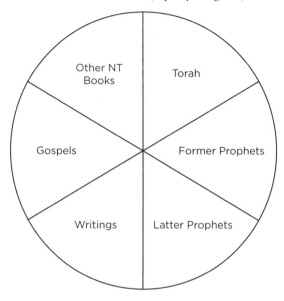

However, before we come to them, we need to consider the time frames over which we are seeking to balance our programs, and we need to think about the place of topical sermons.

## Time Frames

In the discussion above, we have presumed that we want to balance our preaching programs over the course of a single year, and while there is something very natural about connecting with the annual rhythms of our lives, there is no fundamental reason that we cannot offer a balance over a different time frame. If, for example, we decided that we wanted to offer a balance over two years, then we would have around seventeen sermons allocated for each section of Scripture. This would introduce more flexibility for our planning, but also potentially leave longer gaps between sermons from different parts of the Bible. We could also ask if two years is the right period for thinking about balance. Why not three or ten? It is very hard to be definitive about this, and indeed it is not our goal to lay down hard rules, but rather to encourage thoughtful planning based on each preacher's context.

As it happens, we have both had experience working in contexts with large numbers of undergraduate university students. This meant that a pattern we commonly saw was new students arriving at church, staying for three years (the length of many standard undergraduate programs), and then moving away when they finished their degrees. Obviously, this meant that it was essential to have a preaching program that was balanced over a rolling three-year period. If we had been trying to balance out the six parts of Scripture discussed above over such a period, we would have been able to allocate around twenty-six sermons per section over three years, which would have allowed considerable room for flexibility, creativity, and integrity toward the natural shape of the different books of the Bible. Of course, this time frame is very situation-specific and might not be appropriate for churches that do not have a discernible percentage of their members turn over on a regular three-year cycle. Even this cycle might not exist in the same ways any longer, as developments such as the advent of online learning are changing the patterns of participation in tertiary education in many ways.

Again, we believe that it is part of the work of the preacher to figure out the best pattern for his particular context, considering what best serves the needs of his congregation. Just as we would never advocate transcribing someone else's sermon off the internet and delivering it to a congregation (which would be made up of different individuals and different groups of people in different circumstances than the internet preacher's original congregation), neither do we think a preacher can cut and paste his preaching program or even the underlying architectural decisions about that program. This is part of the work of being a vocational preacher, and our hope is simply to help preachers get started in doing the thinking that they have to do freshly for their own ministry settings.

## A Note on Topical Sermons

There is a final consideration for our macro-level thinking before we get down to the brass tacks of planning working preaching programs. It has to do with topical sermons and where they fit in a preaching program. As discussed in chapter 2, by "topical," we mean sermons that are not part of a series teaching through a book of the Bible or necessarily even an exposition of a single passage of Scripture, but that instead explore an issue or theme. The sermon could be properly theological, focusing on a subject such as the love of God or the cross of Jesus. It could also be based on an important felt need, such as healthy relationships, loneliness, or sexuality. Or it might be designed to engage with a contemporary issue, such as science and faith or Islam in Christendom.

Immediately we can see several problems with sermons like these. One is that any passages of Scripture exposited are not presented in the context of the biblical books from which they are taken, so there is a risk of their message being applied only to the question at hand rather than being understood as part of the larger story or argument from which they are abstracted. A second problem is that they steal passages from other sermon series. For example, if the sermon on healthy relationships draws heavily on Ephesians 5:21–33, it will be awkward to come to that passage as part of a later exposition of the book of Ephesians as a whole without needing to preach the same sermon twice. In addition, sometimes it is the climactic passages that are cherry-picked for topical series, so when those texts are reached in an expository series, not only have they already been preached, but a significant dynamic of the whole sequence of sermons can be lost. For example, if there were a topical series on the end times that included a sermon on Revelation 21–22, then a later set of sermons on the book of Revelation might have its dramatic conclusion preempted. Thinking about these things reminds us that if we are trying to preach through the whole Bible in thirty-five years, then in most cases, once we have preached a passage, we should not expect to preach it again.

Another risk with topical sermons is that they can provide the preacher with opportunities to ride his hobby horses, and so to hammer the same issues with far more frequency than they occur in the Bible. In some cases, it is necessary for a preacher to selectively speak to the issues of the age, but this must be balanced against overemphasizing one teaching of the Bible at the expense of the others. In the worst cases, these types of topical sermons might not even engage the Bible much at all. They can end up being less about "What the Bible says about science" and more along the lines of "The pastor's personal reflections on science."

Finally, topical sermons can be jumpy. That is, if they are not based on a single passage of Scripture, they can take the congregation from text to text as an argument is built up. While this might be a necessary part of delivering a systematic theology lecture, it can be unhelpful to a congregation, who might come to believe that this is the right way for the Bible to be read. Rather than modeling a respect for the structural and literary integrity of each book of the Bible, the preacher might end up teaching the congregation that the Bible is best understood by constantly flicking about from place to place.

One reason why pastors preach topical sermons is because they are concerned that their congregations should view the Bible as relevant. While this is a noble concern, it betrays a view that in the form that God gave it to us, the Bible is *not* relevant. The assumption is that following the stories of Israel and the church, the rhythms of the poetry, and the arguments of the apostles as God gave them to us is not as helpful for day-to-day living as hearing specific topics sieved out and presented with more concern for their contemporary significance than their original context. While we are completely committed to contextualized and well-applied preaching, we also believe that what is most formative and beneficial for our people's day-to-day living is for them to be soaked in the text of the Bible as it was given, not just in ideas abstracted from it. We can draw countless practical life lessons from Scripture while allowing it to speak in its own voice. We therefore must not fear that good expository preaching can never shape our congregations for life and godliness in the real world.

Given all that we have said about topical preaching, we would generally choose not to include it in the regular preaching programs of local churches, but to mostly save it for other times in the life of the church (such as retreats or conferences, an idea we will discuss in chap. 9). We would use our weekly sermons to preach expositionally through the books of the Bible using our biblical, systematic, and gospel theologies, and then thoughtfully apply the lessons of each text to the lives of our people. In our next two chapters, we will get down to detail on putting together preaching programs that can achieve this goal.

7

# Choosing Books and Planning Preaching Series

Having established an overall paradigm that divides the Bible into meaningful subsections and that determines what proportion of the preaching program will be allocated to each, the next step is to choose the actual books that will be preached in a given time period. While it is one thing to know that we want to preach, say, nine sermons from the Old Testament Writings in a calendar year, we still need to decide if we will preach through both Ruth and Lamentations, all of Ezra, or a section of the book of Job. Similarly, if we want to preach eight sermons from the New Testament outside of the Gospels, will that mean preaching through 2 and 3 John and Jude; all of Colossians; Acts 1–7; or something else?

## Choosing the Books from Each Section of the Paradigm

Once more, there are no fixed right and wrong answers to be offered at this point, but several considerations should be weighed. First, and perhaps most important, each preacher must understand the particular context into which he will be speaking and the particular needs of the people who will be in the pews. Even two churches in the same town have different histories and different issues before them at any given time. A good preacher should know the flock intimately and have a consciousness of both their immediate circumstances as well as their characterizing values, idols, strengths, and challenges. For example, a church made up of people who are very confident in their salvation as a result of a robust understanding of justification, but who at the same time lack care for one another, might need to hear a series on James. On the other side, a congregation that has a very legalistic approach to being Christian might need to consider Galatians or Romans.

Just as each week's sermon ought to be preached with an awareness of these things, so too should the entire preaching program be shaped with them in mind. This highlights for us again that the work of feeding Jesus's lambs with his word is intensely pastoral and missional, and that it requires the local overseer to be walking closely and sharing life with his people. An internet preacher cannot do this for a congregation, and an internet preaching plan cannot serve them well either.

Second, as noted above, when preparing a preaching program that is part of a long-range plan to preach the whole Bible, we must remember that whatever we plan to preach now we will not plan to preach again. So if we prioritize preaching all of our personal favorite books of the Bible in the first year of our ministry, we should also consider what the diet of Scripture will look like without those books being preached again for the decades that follow. Conversely, whatever we do not preach now we will need to preach later on. So if for some reason we are avoiding a particular book of the Bible, we must remember that the time will come when we have to tackle it and work to deliver it faithfully to the people. For some of us, it might be strange to imagine not returning again to what we have considered to be our stock preaching texts. Perhaps we have worked up a strong series on Ephesians or Romans 1–4 and would like to repreach it sometime—especially if we felt its impact was positive and helpful for the church when we first delivered it. Of course, there may be opportunities for us to repurpose and recycle our old material in new contexts (although good reuse of old texts in new settings can, and probably should, take a lot of extra preparation time), but the ongoing challenge for preachers is to continually be working up strong new sermons from other parts of the Bible.

Third, we would suggest preaching only one book from each subsection of the preaching paradigm at a time. So while we could be true to our paradigm by preaching Isaiah 1–12 one year and Ezekiel 1–11 the next, this would leave our congregation partway through two books of the Latter Prophets at the same time. If we did the same jumping from book to book within the other subsections of our paradigm, we could end up with a dozen or more biblical books left open or bookmarked at the same time. Some people do manage to read many books in parallel and remember where they are in each, but for many this practice can be very confusing because they find it hard to keep track of all the books. Moreover, if we are in the habit of repeatedly launching into new books, we risk creating a potentially unhelpful shape to our long-term program. At worst, we might have a decade when we teach the beginnings of many of the Bible's long books, followed by a decade when we preach all of the middle sections, and then another decade when we approach all of their ends. None of this seems particularly balanced.

We think that a good rule of thumb is to finish preaching through each book that we start before we begin another in the same subcategory. Therefore, if we decide, for example, that we want to preach Luke as our Gospel, we would start at chapter 1 and continue over the years ahead until we came to the end of chapter 24, and only then would we embark on another Gospel. Similarly, if we planned to preach Isaiah as our Latter Prophet, we would start at chapter 1 and keep returning to it in a sequential series until we finished chapter 66. We would not preach partway through Luke and then begin Matthew, or partway through Isaiah and then start with Ezekiel. There are perhaps some exceptions to this rule—in particular, it might be that not too much would be lost if the Psalms and Proverbs were not preached through as whole books, but instead were preached in sermons peppered between other series. However, it is worth noting that in recent times, scholars of the Psalms are recognizing that there is some deliberate structuring of the Psalter as a whole, and Proverbs certainly has a coherent structure that should be respected at least in chapters 1–9.

Finally, it may be worth considering preaching through those multibook parts of the Bible that have a natural sequence in their canonical order. That is, it would seem to make sense to preach through the five books of the Law in sequence, given that each continues on from those that preceded it. Similarly, it could be good to preach through the Former Prophets in order, starting with Joshua in the first year and progressing over time toward the end of 2 Kings. Some might argue that there is nothing to be gained from this level of planning given the extremely long time period over which we are attempting to preach the whole Bible. We could respond that neither is anything lost, but there are, in fact, at least small gains to be made from this approach. Even if few people will have kept the entire narrative alive in their minds over thirty-five years, many will have a real experience of year-to-year continuity, with each year's sermons on the Former Prophets picking up from where this part of the Bible was left off perhaps only twelve months earlier.

### Preaching in Seriatim Series

Throughout this book, we have been working under the conviction that preaching in planned *series* of sermons is far better than preaching lots of stand-alone sermons, even if each of those individual sermons is thoroughly biblical. We have also suggested that one particular type of preaching series is best: the seriatim expository series. Expository preaching is preaching that "exposes" the text of Scripture as it was delivered to us. It does not bring its own agenda to the Bible or to the pulpit, but seeks to understand the Bible texts on their own terms, trusting that God has something to say to his people through them. *Seriatim* is the Latin word for "series"; it conveys the sense of a sequence, distinct from the sense that we sometimes give the word *series* in our preaching programs as merely "a related collection." Seriatim expository preaching therefore aims to preach through each book of the Bible while preserving its God-given fullness and shape.

So while a sermon series titled, say, "Great Heroes of the Bible" certainly engages with Scripture at one level, it could fail to be either expository or seriatim. In this series, heroes such as Abraham, Elijah, and Peter could be discussed synthetically, with the preacher gathering bits of information about them from across various passages in the Bible while never trying to expound any part of the Bible in its own setting. And the sermons as a set would not progressively follow the shape of any book of the Bible. As we have already noted, series like this are problematic in that they do not really respect the way that God chose to give the Bible to us. It is not an oversight that there is no book of "Great Heroes" in the biblical canon; it is not there because God did not intend for us to learn the Bible that way. Rather, the various heroes of the Bible appear at various junctures of the story of God's work in his world, and they are embedded into the context of the biblical books that God gave us. We therefore can actually best understand biblical heroes such as Abraham, Elijah, and Peter when we learn about them in the context of the whole books of Genesis, 1 and 2 Kings, and the Gospels and Acts, respectively.

If whole books of the Bible should be taught in expository seriatim series, it follows that preachers should think not only about preparing individual sermons, but also about preparing whole sermon series. They should not work on their 2 Kings 2:1–18 sermon apart from their broader preparation on the 2 Kings 1–13 series. This allows them to know such things as where the sermon fits into the series; how it follows from the previous sermon and leads into the next; what issues, questions, and themes it will seed, develop, or resolve; and the ways in which these issues, questions, and themes will also be present in other sermons in the series. In short, preachers should prepare each sermon as both a stand-alone message and also as part of a package of sermons that together expound a larger meaningful section of Scripture. Clearly this all takes work, and so just as in the previous chapter we advised setting aside time to plan the preaching paradigm and program, we also recommend scheduling dedicated time to prepare each sermon series on top of the time allocated to prepare each individual sermon.

It is good to recognize that for all the extra work that preaching through the whole Bible requires, there are some significant upsides to preaching the books of the Bible in seriatim expository series. Although the preacher may intuitively think that needing to plan series as well as sermons will eat further into his already stretched time, in practice he may find that he will gain time because of the significant efficiencies in working this way rather than preparing stand-alone sermons week by week. For example, when preparing to preach a series through the whole book of James, the preacher can do just one solid block of work exploring things such as authorship, setting, structure, theological themes, and so on, meaning that this preparation will not need to be done again for each separate sermon in the series. Preparation of the individual sermons should therefore be faster than it would be if they were not part of the series, and the collective time saving across the whole series should be significant. Contrast this to the hypothetical series "Great Heroes of the Bible," for which a responsible preacher would need to do a lot of work to understand Genesis for his sermon on Abraham, a lot of work on 1 and 2 Kings for his Elijah sermon, and a lot of work on the Gospels and Acts (and perhaps 1 and 2 Peter) for his sermon on Peter. This is an enormous amount to take on for one short preaching series.

Not only can time be saved by preaching in series, but the preacher's mind will be more focused too. Rather than flitting from book to book and passage to passage every week, he can immerse himself more thoroughly in one part of the Bible and so allow his thinking to run long and deep in the texts he is preparing to preach. In addition, if he does his series planning weeks or even months before the series is scheduled, he will add in the valuable extra stewing time we discussed at the start of chapter 6. Obviously, all this will also benefit those in the congregation, who are rarely, if ever, able to spend as much time with their minds in the text as the preacher. For them, the less jumping from one part of the Bible to another, the better. Given that we preach for them, not for ourselves, this is a good thing to remember.

## Tackling the Big Books and Creating Series of Series

A challenge we face if we are committed to preaching through whole books of the Bible in seriatim series is the length of some of the books. Most of the Bible's biggest books are in the Old Testament. All five in the Law, along with all in the Former Prophets, are substantial. Isaiah, Jeremiah, and Ezekiel are sometimes collectively called the "Major Prophets" because of their size, and 1 and 2 Chronicles, Job, and Proverbs in the Writings are long too. The shortest of all these is Judges at twenty-one chapters, and the longest is Isaiah with sixty-six—although Jeremiah is longer by verse count. And on top of all of this are the 150 psalms. The New Testament also has several longish books, with Matthew, Luke, John, Acts, and Revelation each exceeding twenty chapters. Also, because of their considerable density, some of the epistles, such as Romans, 1 and 2 Corinthians, and Hebrews can feel quite long too. As we plan to preach these books, their length is perhaps one of the most significant factors in our considerations. In fact, alongside the relative obscurity of some of the larger Old Testament books, their length is probably one of the main reasons that these books are so rarely preached in their entirety (of course, their obscurity may in part be a result of the lack of attention given to them by preachers). It would be nice to find that preachers and their congregations were especially excited by the big books of the Bible for the very fact that they offer so much of God's revelation, but it is very sad, and perhaps a little ironic, that the books in which God has given us most of his words are the books that we tend to listen to the least. It is even sadder to think that this could be the case just because we have never thought through the mechanics and practicalities of teaching these larger books. Too often, we feel stumped as to how we could tackle them, and so we either preach them in overview series or highlights packages (see chap. 3), cherry-pick a key passage for a one-off sermon, or ignore them altogether.

The key to preaching the large books well is to break them down into meaningful sections, similar to the way we can break the Bible down into its various parts. All of the big books of the Bible are made up of sections, many of which are already well recognized by biblical scholars. We only need to take the time for the one-off prework of confirming those section breaks when we first come to preach a big book of the Bible. Then, when we have established the sections, we can take each in turn as the texts for whole sermon series. Section one gives us our text for series one, section two provides our text for series two, and so on. Of course, we do not have to prepare several series from a big book at once. Rather, we can just tackle one section/series at a time as we do our series planning and leave the next section for when we come to prepare the next series, which might not be for another year or more. As we work progressively through the series of series, we will take our congregations through the entire text of the big book.

Some examples might help to illustrate this process. When we come to Genesis, we might recognize that its chapters naturally divide into the following major sections:

Fig. 7.1. Major Sections of Genesis.

| 1-3 | 4-11 | 12-17 | 18-25 | 26-36 | 37-50 |
|-----|------|-------|-------|-------|-------|

The first section, chapters 1 to 3, focuses on creation and humanity's fall into sin. The second records the prepatriarchal period (i.e., the time before the patriarchs, Abraham, Isaac, and Jacob). The chapters in the third section are about the call of Abraham. Section four is on the life of Abraham. Chapters 26–36 follow the stories of Isaac and Jacob. Finally, the last section is the Joseph narrative.

It is important to note that the text itself does not give us hard section breaks. That is, there are no original headings in the book of Genesis that establish these divisions, and the sections are often far more connected than we might sometimes think. For example, the break between Genesis 11 and 12 may not be as stark as it is often presented. Indeed the genealogy in 11:10–26 seems to exist precisely in order to link Abraham with all that comes before. Given this vagueness, each preacher needs to do enough work on the structure of a book as a whole to feel confident that he has identified the most natural breaks. It is also good to notice that in the breakdown presented above, the sections are not of equal length. This is because the goal has been to identify *natural* sections of the text, not to impose artificial divisions. While it would be very neat to divide Genesis into five sections of ten chapters each, this would not reflect the structure of the narrative in any meaningful way.

Having determined the macrostructure of the book of Genesis, we can set to work on making the first section into a series of sermons that will go toward our seasonal preaching of the Law.

Then, when we return to preach from the Law again in twelve, twenty-four, or however many months our paradigm prescribes, we will begin working on our series on Genesis 4–11, and so on. For Exodus, we might determine that the chapters naturally divide into the following major sections:[1]

Fig. 7.2. Major Sections of Exodus.

| 1–4 | 5–11 | 12:1–15:21 | 15:22–18:27 | 19–24 | 25–31 | 32–34 | 35–40 |
|-----|------|------------|-------------|-------|-------|-------|-------|

We notice here that there are more subsections of Exodus than Genesis, despite the fact that Exodus is a shorter book. This means that the preacher either will need to preach more sermon series on Exodus than Genesis—even if there are fewer sermons in each series—or consider combining some sequential sections to make for longer series. Perhaps the section comprising 12:1–15:21, which covers the exodus from Egypt itself, could be combined with the following section comprising 15:22–18:27, which tracks the events between the exodus and the arrival at Mount Sinai. (A series covering these sections together could be descriptively named "From Egypt to Sinai.") It might be possible to make similar decisions for other sections of Exodus, or for adjacent sections of other big books of the Bible.

Some of the long books of the Bible are harder to subdivide. The Psalter is one example. It is something of a special case because it is not narratival and because each of the psalms has considerable stand-alone integrity. To be sure, there is some macrostructure in the Psalter, the most obvious being its division into five books, or subcollections of psalms, and another being the grouping of similar psalms, such as the psalms of ascent (Pss. 120–134) or the hallelujah psalms (Pss. 146–150) that close the book. Scholars also recognize different types of psalms, such as the psalms of individual lament, the psalms of corporate lament, the wisdom psalms, and

---

1. An alternative breakdown for Exodus 20–31 is given in Fig. 8.4, pp. 172–73.

so on. While these categorizations can be helpful, we must be careful not to overvalue them, as they are not designated as groups or types in the text itself. When preaching through the Psalter, we therefore have much more freedom and flexibility than with most of the other long books. This means that it could be quite appropriate to preach a series of almost any length from the Psalter, and perhaps even to take different psalms from across the Psalter when doing so rather than always taking a number of sequential psalms.

It might be helpful to make two comments about this flexibility. First, it means that sermons on psalms could be used to gap fill a preaching program. That is, if a circumstance arises where a preaching calendar has a spare week or two, choosing to preach psalms at that point would not reject the integrity of biblical books in the way that preaching other one-off sermons might. Of course, we must be careful never to see the psalms solely as gap fillers in a purely functional sense or to become lazy planners who overuse the psalms to plug holes in our preaching calendars. We must plan to preach the psalms thoughtfully, respecting them as precious parts of God's word, not just conveniences, and we must work hard on our preaching programs to minimize gaps, even if that means recasting them and even going back to square one several times. At the risk of repeating too often what we have said before, this is all part of the necessary work of the vocational preaching pastor.

Second, if we choose to create series comprising nonsequential psalms, we ought to have a good rationale for doing so and a good sense of the long-term implications of that decision. There may be a logic to crafting a sermon series that takes us from a lament psalm to a royal psalm to a hallelujah psalm, but every time we pick an ideal psalm to contribute to a bigger point, we remove the option of preaching that psalm in the future.

Another alternative for preaching the psalms is to use them similarly to the way that the New Testament uses them. It is very clear that the early Christians held the Psalter in very high regard and not only sang the psalms (Eph. 5:19), but also used them to shape their theological thinking. Indeed, Jesus and the New Testament as a whole quote the Psalms more than any other Old Testament book, and only five New Testament books do not contain references or allusions to the Psalms. Given that the New Testament Christians invariably used the Psalms to support and strengthen the cause and message of the gospel, perhaps we could preach an appropriate psalm as a one-off sermon at the end of a New Testament sermon series. The most obvious examples would be to preach Psalm 22 after a series on Matthew's Gospel that had included chapter 27, where Jesus cries out with the opening line of that psalm, or Psalm 110 after a series on Acts that covered Acts 2, where Peter quotes from it. Once more, however, thoughtfulness is needed when making these decisions. Peter also quotes Psalm 16 in Acts 2, and Psalm 110 is also quoted in Matthew 22 and Hebrews 1, meaning that pastors need to make sensible decisions about the point at which they will preach these psalms.

A final possibility is to intersperse relevant psalms into other sermon series when they are directly related. For example, the psalms that refer to David's activities could be incorporated into series on the books of Samuel at the points where those activities are reached in the narrative.

These approaches are possible and could be very helpful, but they would require very careful planning. On balance, many preachers may decide that it makes the best sense to preach the Psalms in their biblical sequence, even if they cannot always see a strong connection between one psalm and the next. God has overseen their compilation into their existing order, and we can trust that he can use it for his purposes.

### A Brief Note on Genre

Discussion of the Psalter as a unique type of big Bible book leads us to briefly consider the importance of understanding genre for preaching. A text's genre is critical to its purpose, and this fact is too often overlooked when it comes to the books of the Bible. Some preachers' view of genre is that it is little more than a stylistic feature of the text that we need to see through in order to get to the underlying meaning or doctrines. On this assessment, genre is incidental to, rather than constitutive of, the text. But the reality is that a text's genre is an essential and inseparable part of its meaning and purpose. Narrative cannot communicate timeless emotion in the way that psalmic poetry does. Poetry cannot discuss details of occasional community issues in the ways that a letter does. A letter cannot paint terrifyingly glorious pictures of the end times in the way that apocalyptic writing does. Apocalyptic writing cannot bring context-specific warnings in the way that prophecy does. And prophecy cannot generate empathetic perspective in the way that narrative does. The genre of the books of the Bible are of great consequence—they are a literary feature that is a God-intended part of the written word.

Of course, we know much of this intuitively. No one would try to preach through the Psalter as though it were a continuous narrative. However, some preachers do have a tendency to treat every text like a Pauline epistle, and so are always looking for the argument or absolute propositions it contains. But some texts (including some of Paul's!) were not written to argue propositions, and to take that as their purpose would be to get them wrong.

Because of the importance of genre for meaning, we encourage all preachers to spend some time developing a good understanding of the different biblical genres—not just their form, but their function too—as they prepare to preach from the different books of the Bible, large and small.[2]

---

2. For a good introduction to the function and purposes of the biblical genres, see Kevin J. Vanhoozer, *Is There a Meaning in This Text? The Bible, the Reader, and the Morality of Literary Knowledge* (Leicester, UK: Apollos, 1998), 335–50. For discussion on the importance of genre to preaching, see Ian Hussey, ed., *Preaching with an Accent: Biblical Genres for Australian Congregations* (Sydney: Morling Press, 2020).

# 8

# Putting Preachable Texts into the Calendar

Having set a long-term paradigm and decided on the particular books of the Bible that we will preach over a given period of time, the next step is to work out how many sermons we will need to preach through each book or each section of a book. We may have decided to preach through Exodus 1–4 for our Law sermons and through 1 Thessalonians for our Acts/Epistles sermons, but how many sermons will there be in each of those series?

A great temptation is to force the text to fit the number of preaching weeks we have available; if there are nine weeks allocated to Law, it would be very helpful if our Exodus series fell neatly into nine sermons. But of course, this puts us at risk of artificially dividing the texts rather than looking for the natural breaks and sections. We may find that a mismatch between the number of sermons in our series and the number of preaching slots means we need to rethink parts of our calendar several times over. We need to be both flexible and determined at this point—flexible enough to realize that our plans will often not be as tidy as we would like, but determined enough to keep striving for the ideal shape to our program as far as that is possible.

At this point, we see again the great importance of setting aside good time to do concrete midrange planning. We need this so that we can study the text carefully and discern the natural preachable passages, and also to carefully massage our preaching calendars so that they square with the sermon series as much as possible. If we do not do this planning well in advance of preaching the series, we might find out too late that the book or book section divides into more or fewer sermons than we had anticipated, but we have not left ourselves enough time to rearrange things to account for this. In a pressured situation like this, we are more likely to compromise the integrity of the sermon series than we would be if we had more space to think our timetables through again. Dividing our series into sermons again requires that we plan to plan.

## Dividing Books, or Book Sections, into Preachable Passages

When dividing books of the Bible or sections of big books of the Bible into preachable passages, we must remember that in many instances, the chapter divisions of the Bible are not helpful. "One chapter, one sermon" sounds neat and tidy, but it actually can be quite unhelpful. There are some exceptions, such as the book of Ruth, where the four chapters clearly break the book into its four distinct parts, or the Psalms, where each psalm is a coherent whole, but this is not the case for the whole Bible. The Bible was divided into chapters in medieval times, and because many of the chapters are roughly equal in length, they can be helpful if we want to do things such as read the Bible for a certain period of time each day. So if we have set aside fifteen minutes of our daily quiet time for Bible reading, we might reasonably aim to read three chapters per day. This is simple and appropriate for our personal devotions, when we may not want to spend too much time thinking about the best divisions of each book and when we will pick up where we had left off just twenty-four hours earlier. But when we are working to exposit coherent blocks of Scripture to others who will be taught this way only once a week, we need to recognize that the Bible's often artificial chapter breaks can be unhelpful to us.

Similarly, the section headings offered in most modern English translations are not always correct. In some cases, they do helpfully show us where the text moves from one section to another or where a chapter break should be ignored, but in some cases they are misjudged too. A quite unhelpful heading was the one that was put between 1 Corinthians 10:33 and 11:1, coinciding with the chapter break, in the New American Standard Bible. This made it seem as though Paul's injunction to imitate him as he imitated Christ leads into his discussions on head coverings in church instead of concluding his thoughts on Christian liberty. Like the chapterization of the Bible, the headings are not original, but have been added in by translators and publishers as aids to the reader. The headings can actually be even more unhelpful than the chapter breaks because even when they do rightly recognize a break in the text, they might not correctly label the content of what follows. For example, many English Bibles title Exodus 15 "The Song of Moses," even though verse 1 of that chapter says that "Moses *and the people of Israel*" sang the song together. It is a small point at one level, yet it could still set up some casual readers to think that it was only Moses, and not the whole nation, who praised God after he saved Israel through the Red Sea. We also know that we shouldn't put too much stock in the headings in our Bibles when we see all the places where the translators have labeled sections of the Pentateuch "Miscellaneous Laws" or similar. This is a sure sign that even if they have made an excellent translation, those who put the headings in place did not come to a definitive understanding of the structure or unity of the content in those parts of the Scriptures.

After having read and thought about it, a good way for a preacher to start getting a handle on the natural sections of a book of the Bible is to have a look at the breakdowns that are offered in the introductions of the commentaries on that book. These offer us a macrounderstanding of the shape of the whole book, and we lose some of the real value of our commentaries when we only flip them open to the particular passages we are studying. So while it may be helpful to mine a commentator's insight, knowledge, and wisdom about, say, 1 Thessalonians 2, we also need to know whether the author thinks 1 Thessalonians 2 is a meaningful unit of 1 Thessalonians (no one does). We need to understand how the letter naturally divides if we are to preach sensible, coherent passages of text.

Having suggested turning to the commentaries for guidance, we need to acknowledge what some have immediately thought: the commentaries do not all agree about the structure of the books of the Bible (and much more besides). Unfortunately, this is unavoidably true, and it reminds us that commentaries are only ever to be used as helpful guides, and never to be taken with equivalent authority to Scripture itself. Commentaries need to be considered and critically evaluated, and we always need to read through the commentator's justification for his or her structural outline of the book of the Bible with careful reference to the Bible itself rather than just swallowing whatever is offered without discernment. In some cases, we may be convinced that the commentator has it right. In others, we may not.

One thing we can do to help make our own evaluations is to line up the analysis offered by one commentator with those made by others. If we see great consistency in their assessments, we might be more likely to conclude that the first commentator's decisions were right. If, on the other hand, there is little agreement, we might see a need to prayerfully investigate the Bible book more carefully ourselves in order to determine which analysis of it seems best. Below is an example of this kind of comparison of perceived structures of 1 Thessalonians, with the section breaks indicated by dashed lines:[1]

---

1. Taken from F. F. Bruce, *1 & 2 Thessalonians* (Waco, TX: Word, 1982), 4; Leon Morris, *1 and 2 Thessalonians: An Introduction and Commentary*, rev. ed. (Leicester, UK: Inter-

Fig. 8.1. Scholarly Divisions of 1 Thessalonians.

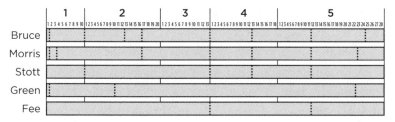

When we look at this comparison, we immediately notice that there is both good agreement and significant disagreement between the scholars. In most cases, neat breaks are recognized between chapters 1 and 2; chapters 3 and 4; verses 12 and 13 of chapter 4; and verses 11 and 12 of chapter 5. But there is less agreement on any breaks within chapters 2 and 3, or at the end of chapter 5. Given this, we might confidently accept some of the widely recognized section breaks without too much complication, but see the need to confirm others as we divide this book into the separate passages that we will preach from.

There are a few questions that might be helpful to ask when further considering how a book naturally divides. If it is narrative, it is worth asking, "Where do the different 'scenes' start and end?" By asking this sort of question, we recognize that John 7–8 (excluding 7:53–8:11; see chap. 2) is one long scene in which Jesus is attending the Festival of Booths in Jerusalem. It is quite helpful to notice this unit of text, as the structure of John 2–11 can be very hard to discern. If we are preparing to preach an epistle, we might ask, "When is there a change of topic?" In 1 Corinthians, this is an easy question to answer, because Paul has formulaically introduced several of his topics with the phrase "Now concerning . . ." Noting these markers in the text helps us to recognize that while chapter 7 has a certain

---

Varsity, 1984), 38–39; John R. W. Stott, *The Message of Thessalonians: The Gospel and the End of Time* (Leicester, UK: Inter-Varsity, 1991), 7; Gene L. Green, *The Letters to the Thessalonians* (Grand Rapids, MI: Eerdmans, 2002), viii–ix; Gordon D. Fee, *The First and Second Letters to the Thessalonians* (Grand Rapids, MI: Eerdmans, 2009), v–vi.

unity about it—it has to do with marital relationships—it can also be rightly thought of as two passages, the first about the goodness of marriage ("Now concerning . . . ," v. 1ff.) and the second about widows and single people ("Now concerning the betrothed . . . ," v. 25ff.). Although not quite as straightforward, this kind of question can also help us in our work of understanding the structure of 1 Thessalonians. If we think about that letter in terms of the topics it addresses, we see that the middle sections are focused on faith, love, and hope, which is a common triplet for Paul, although here it is not in its standard order of faith, hope, and love (e.g., 1 Cor. 13:13).[2] Instead, the order matches two verses that almost bookend the letter: 1:3 and 5:8. With this understanding, we might feel confident to finalize our division of the letter into the following six passages:

Fig. 8.2. Alternative Divisions of 1 Thessalonians.

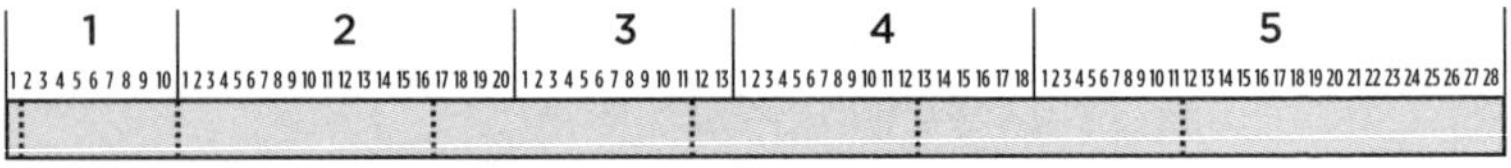

This gives us a six-sermon series, with the following texts and emphases:

1:1–10—the Thessalonians' conversion
2:1–16—Paul's model of ministry
2:17–3:11—Paul's concern for the Thessalonians' faith
3:12–4:12—how Christians should love one another
4:13–5:11—Christian hope
5:12–28—corporate life

Having done this work, the preacher then knows that he ideally needs a block of six weeks in which to preach his 1 Thessalonians series, and he can then turn to thinking about the best options for building that into his working program.

---

2. The "standard" order may not be so standard, with Colossians 1:4–5 also speaking of faith, love, and hope.

The point here is not to offer an indisputable structural analysis of 1 Thessalonians, but to give an example of the kind of structural work that a preacher needs to do when planning what to preach and how that work might bear fruit. Once again, we should note that, at this point, no work at all has been done to prepare any individual sermons. On the one hand, this reminds us of the extra work it will take to plan to preach through the entire Bible. On the other hand, we should be excited about how obviously this prework is going to help us when we come to prepare each sermon, and how good it will be for the church to sit under a well-designed 1 Thessalonians series as part of its ongoing diet of Scripture.

Another question that we might add to the two already suggested to help determine the natural breaks in biblical books is "What is the applyable unit of text?" This really is a preacher's question, as it requires thinking forward through the exegesis of the text and on to application for those who will hear the text expounded. Again, the 1 Thessalonians example is very helpful to us here, as we see that each of the sections identified above would have a clear application. If the book were preached a chapter at a time, application would be very confused, as there would be the need to apply both Paul's model of ministry and his concern for faith in the sermon on chapter 2, and then his concern for faith would need to be reapplied in the sermon on chapter 3 along with part of his teaching on loving relationships. Once more we see that the chapterization of the Bible can be quite unhelpful for us.

## How Much Text and Time per Sermon?

In working out meaningful passages of Scripture to preach—and as we recognize that just a chapter per sermon may not be ideal—we come to the question of whether there is an ideal length for each passage of the Bible that will be preached. The short answer is yes, there is an *ideal* length, but not a *uniform* length. That is, the ideal length is however long the coherent section of text is, and that varies from passage to passage. Some passages are of a length that many churches are used to, such as 2 Samuel 2:1–11. But others are not. The obvious examples are Psalm 117 and Psalm 119. If we consider each of the psalms to be equivalent to a chapter, these are respectively the shortest and longest chapters of the Bible; the first is just two verses, and the second is 176. But both have independent literary integrity, and therefore it would not seem appropriate to preach Psalm 117 along with another text in the same sermon or to divide Psalm 119 into lots of sermons so that it is effectively chopped up (or even butchered). Just as we trust that God superintended all of the content of Scripture, so too we believe that he is sovereign over the length of every coherent unit of text. We therefore need to respect Psalms 117 and 119 by preaching each as it stands without addition or division.

This leads us to ask a related question, which may, in fact, be the single most contentious question in all of the church today: "How long should a sermon be?" Most churches at least have an implicit answer to this question, if not a clearly stated expectation, and there tends to be a great commitment to—and enforcement of—the law of sermon length within any given congregation. But even as fixed as this length may be within a church, different churches can have very different norms for sermon length. Some churches always and only have a sermon that is less than ten minutes long; others standardly allot thirty to thirty-five minutes. Some are precise: twenty-two minutes, no more, no less. Having a predictable sermon length is quite understandable when the whole church service is running to a schedule. It would be quite unmanageable for families if sermons regularly went far too long and caused the whole service to run overtime, meaning that no reliable plan could be made for lunch, weekend sports, or babies' naps. Conversely, it would be a little embarrassing if a Christmas Eve vigil that was meant to run from eleven o'clock until midnight—and therefore take the congregation into the break of Christmas Day—ended fifteen minutes early because the sermon was unexpectedly brief (something that perhaps one of us has had personal experience with).

But do these concerns necessarily mean that all sermons should be the same length? Of course, the great problem with this expectation is that it presumes that all parts of God's word can, and should, be expounded in exactly the same amount of time, which is clearly not the case. If we were to couple this thinking to our commitment to preach coherent units of Scripture, we might end up needing to include a great deal of padding in our Psalm 117 sermon and to race through our Psalm 119 sermon at breakneck speed. In both cases, we would be prioritizing the semiarbitrary time constraints put on us by our church culture over the needs of the word before us or the people to whom we are bringing it. It would seem far more sensible to simply allow for sermons of different length—whatever length is necessary to helpfully and adequately expound and apply the coherent passage of Scripture we are preaching. If we make this decision, we will feel more comfortable preaching a five-minute sermon on Psalm 117, a twenty-two-minute sermon on Psalm 118, and an hourlong sermon on Psalm 119.

Immediately we see at least two consequences of taking this approach to preaching. The first is that we may need to develop as preachers who are competent to preach good sermons of significantly different lengths. There are major challenges in preparing and preaching both great short sermons and engaging long sermons, and further challenges in growing into a preacher who can do both and knows which is required when. This is all part of the ongoing personal development that is necessary for every lifelong vocational preacher (which we will consider further in chap. 11).

The second consequence of letting the text set the sermon length is that we need to know how to prepare edifying church services that are flexible enough to account for sermons of different lengths. Although it creates challenges, this prioritization of the ministry of the word in the service can actually make for more powerful and integrated corporate gatherings. So while it may be that our sermon on Psalm 117 is short, the rest of the service could serve as an immediate application of the teaching of that passage. The psalm is almost nothing more than an exhortation to praise the Lord, and so it would seem entirely appropriate if, after hearing that message, the congregation shared in an extended time of corporate praise. The leaders could plan to sing twice as many songs as normal, and perhaps even to allow a period of time for members of the church to call out public statements of praise to God too. These things would not only fill out the service, they would also put into practice, and thereby reinforce, the message of the psalm. Things might be different two weeks later when Psalm 119 is preached. It might even be that the Bible reading and the sermon together take up 90 percent or more of the service time and that other things are limited, or even not included at all. But again, this could actually honor the teaching of the psalm, which is all about the preciousness, beauty, and desirability of the word of God above all else. This truth is only magnified when it is proclaimed through a church service that does little more than soak the congregation in the words of the very psalm that brings it to us.

The difference between the length of Psalms 117 and 119 is stark, but not unique for different preaching texts. Some preachers might choose to preach a single sermon covering all of the plagues that are recounted in Exodus 7:14–10:29, and this would be a sermon of a very different length compared to one on the baptism of Jesus in Luke 3:21–22. Similarly, the temple vision of Ezekiel 40–48 and the record of Shamgar in Judges 3:31 would make for sermons that run to different times. However, the points are the same for all: careful midrange planning is necessary not only to balance the congregation's diet of Scripture, but also to understand the preachable units of the books of the Bible we are preaching and to enable the planning of appropriate services in which the sermons will be preached. This sounds like a lot of work, but perhaps it is helpful to recognize that many churches already do this at least for their services at Christmas and Easter. Commonly, those gatherings have sermons of different lengths in the expectation that different people will be present than the weekly church members, and they are also often very carefully crafted so that the preaching text dovetails with lots of related service content. The challenge is whether something similar can be done for each text and each preaching day, and to thereby respect and magnify the word of God in all of its diversity. We will return to this idea in the second half of chapter 9.

A final point on identifying the right unit of text for preaching is that there are, in fact, different ways that passages can be legitimately divided, or rather, there are different levels of detail at which we can choose to preach a text. A good example of this comes from Ephesians 5:22–6:9. This is a coherent unit of text that expounds the requirement of 5:21 for Christians to submit to one another out of reverence for Christ. Therefore, it would respect the integrity of the text to preach a sermon on this passage as a whole. However, it is also true that the passage can be further divided into three distinct subsections: (1) 5:22–33, addressing the relationship between husbands and wives; (2) 6:1–4, addressing the relationship between children and parents; and (3) 6:5–9, addressing the relationship between bondservants and masters. On the one hand, it could be considered a little redundant to preach one sermon for each of these subsections, as all draw on the same principles and similar paradigms. On the other hand, there are many good reasons to do so: different human relationships should be addressed differently; these texts have been used to justify terrible abuse that needs to be acknowledged and rejected; there are some interpretive debates that may need to be addressed because of our congregation's prior engagement with them; many people have no picture of these relational dynamics functioning well, so they need to be helpfully illustrated; these teachings cut against some of the major currents of today's culture; and so on. It is possible to treat many other texts at different levels of detail too, and a good rule of thumb is that we should preach passages of Scripture that are large enough to capture overarching connections but small enough that we have time to go into all their details and important issues. In many cases, pastoral wisdom and insight are required to determine the right level for a given congregation.

## What to Do with the Bible's Repetition

In addition to determining the right length of passage to preach from, preachers also need to work out how they will deal with the considerable repetition in the Bible. It is hard to escape the fact that there are many places where the Bible goes over the same ground more than once, and it may at first feel tedious to prepare sermons on texts that are essentially the same as others, and redundant to preach them. (For some reason, this problem is not always felt by those preachers who preach the same text over and over rather than preaching through the whole Bible.)

We saw that there is a degree of repetition in Ephesians 5:21–6:9. Another great example of repetition in the Bible can be found in Acts 10 and 11, where verses 9–16 of the first chapter are closely recounted again in verses 5–10 of the second. (Interestingly, these passages also report a summary of repetitive events. Acts 10:16 and 11:10 both say, "This happened three times . . .") Given that these texts are in consecutive chapters, some preachers might be tempted to either preach all of Acts 10 and 11 in one sermon—thereby avoiding the need to repeat themselves one week later—or perhaps to skip over the repetitive part of chapter 11 after having given their exposition of all of chapter 10. While the temptation to do either of those things can be understood, perhaps neither would be the right decision. A high view of the Bible must recognize that even its repetition is God-ordained. The fact that two consecutive chapters contain similar material is not an artifact of poor editing by Luke, but part of God's deliberate design of his Scriptures. For some reason, he wanted the same thing to be heard twice in relatively quick succession. The faithful preacher will therefore preach both texts fully, and in so doing, communicate not just the truth of the texts but their balance too.

There might be several reasons that God built so much repetition into the Scriptures. One is that repetition helps to cement truths in our minds; the more we hear something, the more it gets lodged in our memories. Another is that having something we already know recounted helps us call it back to the front of our minds. The Scriptures do make it clear that it is not adequate for God's people to simply memorize things; we must keep gospel truths ever present in our conscious minds, and repetition of those truths is a way to help us do that. Repetition can also serve to cast a slightly different light on something if the setting in which it comes is different. So, for example, it is one thing for God's people to hear of his unfailing love as they go through periods of oppression, and it is another to hear of that unfailing love when their own sin has been exposed.

In our Acts 10 and 11 example, the message was so radical for Jewish ears that the quick repetition may have been intended partly to help the news sink in for the first readers. Hearing God say that he had now made acceptable foods that had been prohibited under the Mosaic Law, and by analogy that Gentiles could receive the Spirit and be counted among the people of God, was nearly unimaginable to many first-century Jews.

On closer inspection, it is also apparent that the two accounts have some significant differences and come to us in different contexts. The first comes as part of Luke's narrative of the gospel advancing to the Gentiles, and in it, Peter is referred to in the third person. The second is found in Peter's defense speech, given in response to the accusations of the Judaizing party (those Jewish Christians who believed that Gentile converts to Christianity had to become Messianic Jews, that is, be converted to Judaism as well as to Christ). Thus, it is a short apologetic recorded in the first person; the story that Peter was a part of in chapter 10 has become part of the message he proclaims in chapter 11. Someone preaching carefully through the whole text of Acts would have the opportunity to highlight both the strong connections and the important differences between these two passages, as well as the significance of each in the story of the early advance of the gospel through the Roman world.

Of course, when we are thinking about repetition in the Bible, we cannot help but remember that the two books of Samuel and the two books of Kings parallel the two books of Chronicles, or that we have four separate Gospels. These are examples of far more than passage-level repetition (although they also contain much of that), but are entire books that each take us through much of the same story and history.

In the Gospels, we have overlapping accounts of Jesus's incarnation, earthly ministry, passion, and resurrection, and so sometimes when preachers expound the Gospels, they seek to harmonize them. Harmonization involves working out how each passage of a Gospel fits not just within its own structure, but also into the accounts provided by the other Gospels. A classic harmonization problem is the story of Jesus's cleansing of the temple, which in John's Gospel occurs at the beginning of his ministry (John 2:13–22), but in Matthew's happens at the end (Matt. 21:12–17). While all evangelical commentators agree that the event really took place, some say that one of the two Gospel writers stylistically crafted his source materials into a story that was shaped around his theological concerns rather than the original chronology. Others simply say that there were two separate temple-cleansing incidents that topped and tailed Jesus's ministry. It is certainly worth preachers spending some time thinking these types of issues through. However, it is perhaps more important that in their preaching, they focus on the text before them and not spend too much time on other texts that may or may not harmonize with it. This helps keep the congregation focused on the texts as they were written and ensures that a sermon from a series on one Gospel does not spend too much time engaging with the texts of the others. Ultimately, while harmonization can help us think well about the sequence of events in Jesus's life and ministry, and about the development of the Gospels as texts, it does run the risk of taking us away from the books of the Bible as texts with standalone integrity and from the intent of their authors in writing the works they did.

Adding our thoughts on repetition to our earlier comments about genre, it is interesting to note that in some books of the Bible, repetition can be accompanied by a switch in genre. A great example is the story of the Israelites crossing the Red Sea as part of their flight from Egypt. In Exodus 14, the event of the crossing is narrated, then it is celebrated in song in chapter 15. The content of these two chapters is much the same, but the very fact that it is repeated points to its importance. That it is repeated after the people have been delivered means that it can take on a more thankful and joyful tone, and its translation into verse gives it a more timeless and memorable quality for the people. Songs are not created to be sung just once, but over and over again. There is therefore much to say from Exodus 15 that isn't just a straight rehash of Exodus 14, and both chapters should be preached as part of the work of teaching the whole book of Exodus.

## Mapping Out the Year(s)

Having thought about dividing the text of Scripture into its natural preachable passages, we can now think more about populating our preaching calendar. We have spoken a number of times about our preaching calendar without yet giving any detail of what it actually is. What does it look like? How do we set it out? How do we use it? While there are, once more, no strict rules, the preaching calendar we envisage is simply a large table that lays out the upcoming preaching program. It could be nothing more than an existing calendar with the sermon texts written in on the upcoming Sundays, but this probably will not be as helpful to us as something purposely designed. Below, we offer a straightforward spreadsheet layout that we feel makes for a useful basic preaching calendar. There are many ways it could be developed and modified to increase its usefulness, so what we have here is meant to be only a guide or starting point. Although some people still prefer to work with pen and paper, we suggest keeping the preaching calendar in electronic format, as this enables instant statistics and easy sharing with others.

The first step is simply to create a column listing all the upcoming Sundays—and other teaching days, such as Good Friday—for the coming year, or for whatever period you have decided to balance your preaching program. It is always a good idea to do this work long before reaching the end of the current preaching program—say, with six months to go—so that you do not feel as though you need to rush the process to have something in place for next weekend. The next step is to mark out all of the important dates in the year that are beyond your control. These will differ for each ministry context; for example, school holidays and public holidays vary from place to place. Others dates, such as Christmas, Easter, and New Year's Day, are more universal, although Easter, of course, changes each year. Following this, you can also mark in the dates that have particular importance to your congregation. These might be one-off events, such as a significant anniversary of one of the church's ministries, or they might be events that come in regular patterns, such as the days of the liturgical seasons or the annual midyear mission trip.

Once all of these are in place, you can start to get a sense for the size of the blocks of consecutive teaching weeks that are available to you. This is important when thinking about preaching sermons in series, as there are times when it can be very helpful to fit sermon series into specific periods on the calendar. For example, if your church observes liturgical seasons, it could make a lot of sense to see if you can preach a six-week-long sermon series through Lent. Or if you have a large number of families with school-aged children, there might be reasons to line up sermon series with the school terms, if that is possible. To work out exactly what blocks of time you will work with, you need to make some judgments. For example, you may find that a school term is shorter one year due to a holiday; therefore, if you want to match your sermon series to the school terms, you will have only a four-week block in that term. However, you might also decide that the school term is largely irrelevant to your planning, and so you are comfortable scheduling a continuous series from that term into the vacation, and so on.

At this stage, your calendar should look something like this (note that this calendar reflects school and holiday schedules in our ministry context of Australia):

Fig. 8.3. Annual Preaching Calendar.

| MONTH | DATE | NOTES | MONTH | DATE | NOTES |
|---|---|---|---|---|---|
| Jan. | 4 | | Jul. | 5 | |
| | 11 | School holidays | | 12 | School holidays |
| | 18 | | | 19 | |
| | 25 | School holidays + long weekend | | 26 | |
| Feb. | 1 | | Aug. | 2 | |
| | 8 | | | 9 | |
| | 15 | Lent starts Wed 18 | | 16 | |
| | 22 | | | 23 | |
| | | | | 30 | |
| Mar. | 1 | | Sep. | 6 | Father's Day |
| | 8 | Public holiday long weekend | | 13 | |
| | 15 | | | 20 | |
| | 22 | | | 27 | School holidays |
| | 29 | Palm Sunday | Oct. | 4 | School holidays + long weekend |
| Apr. | 2 | Maundy Thursday | | 11 | School holidays |
| | 3 | Good Friday | | 18 | |
| | 5 | Easter Day (End Daylight Saving) | | 25 | |
| | 12 | School holidays | Nov. | 1 | |
| | 19 | | | 8 | |
| | 26 | School holidays + long weekend | | 15 | |
| May | 3 | | | 22 | |
| | 10 | Mother's Day | | 29 | Advent starts |
| | 17 | | Dec. | 6 | |
| | 24 | Pentecost | | 13 | School holidays |
| | 31 | | | 20 | |
| Jun. | 7 | | | 24 | School holidays/Christmas Eve |
| | 14 | | | 25 | School holidays/Christmas Day |
| | 21 | (Ramadan prayers start Thu 18) | | 26 | School holidays/Christmas Day 2 |
| | 28 | | | 27 | School holidays |
| | | | Jan. | 3 | School holidays + long weekend |
| | | | | 10 | School holidays |

With something like this, we can immediately get a sense of the shape of the year and how that might affect our preaching. If we do decide that working around school holidays is important, we can see that we have a twelve-sermon block from February through early April, but also that the end of that block is Easter. We can see that the rest of April might be a good time for a three-sermon series—perhaps some psalms—before moving into another nine-week block. With these kinds of observations in mind, we can turn back to the prework we did on the books of the Bible we are planning to preach and start thinking about what will fit best where. When we have made our decisions, we can extend the table to include our series texts and even working sermon titles. Below, on pages 172–173, is an example of this where we are continuing with series in the long books of Exodus and John, and where we have decided that the school holidays are not fully determinative of our plans.

Taking the time to develop a program like this brings great blessing to churches that are committed to sitting under the word of God. It all happens before any actual sermon preparation is done, but it charts a course for the church that will take the people deep and far through the word. If a preacher takes time out each year to populate this calendar for the upcoming twelve months, he will be doing a fantastic job of meeting his obligation to feed the flock on the whole counsel of God and to thereby grow them toward maturity in Christ. We cannot recommend this work strongly enough.

There is, however, even more that can be done with a calendar like this. For example, it can be used as the backbone of an entire integrated discipleship program for the whole church that might include ministry to children, Bible study groups, and outreach. We will explore some of these possibilities and the benefits of having a set of programs integrated around the preaching calendar in the next chapter. The table can also be extended a little to generate some useful data that will help with ongoing planning. By adding in columns to record the subsection of Scripture from which the sermon text comes and who the preacher is, we can make tallies or graphs that help us see if our plans match our commitments. The nice thing about doing this in an electronic spreadsheet is that we can very quickly test lots of possibilities and see the balance that they give us. Live calculations, tables, and graphs are very easy to set up these days and are standard features in all the common office software packages, but if you do not feel confident to do this, you might find that there are members of your congregation who work in offices or who are high school students who can help you.

We will return to this calendar again in chapter 10, but having now laid it out, we will move on to part 3 and to think more broadly about some attendant matters that arise when we set out to preach the whole Bible.

Fig. 8.4. Annual Preaching Calendar (with Texts and Sermon Titles).

| MONTH | DATE | NOTES | SERIES | TEXT | TITLE |
|---|---|---|---|---|---|
| Jan. | 4 | | Joel: Returning to God | Joel 1:1–2:17 | Sin's Price & Pain |
| | 11 | School holidays | | Joel 2:18–27 | Healing & Wholeness |
| | 18 | | | Joel 2:28–3:17 | The Day of the Lord |
| | 25 | School holidays + long weekend | | Joel 3:18–21 | Hope for God's People |
| Feb. | 1 | | John 7–8: Jesus in Public | John 7:1–24 | Meeting Expectations? |
| | 8 | | | John 7:25–36 | Knowing God, Going to God |
| | 15 | Lent starts Wed 18 | | John 7:37–52 | Search and You Will See |
| | 22 | | | John 8:12–20 | God on His Side |
| Mar. | 1 | | | John 8:21–30 | Two Ways to Die |
| | 8 | Public holiday long weekend | | John 8:31–38 | The Truth Will Set You Free |
| | 15 | | | John 8:39–59 | Deadly Relationships |
| | 22 | | Ephesians: One in Christ | Eph. 1:1–14 | Every Spiritual Blessing |
| | 29 | Palm Sunday | | Eph. 1:15–23 | Called into Hope |
| Apr. | 2 | Maundy Thursday | | | *No sermon* |
| | 3 | Good Friday | | Eph. 2:1–10 | Saved by Grace |
| | 5 | Easter Day (End Daylight Saving) | | Eph. 2:11–22 | One (Temple?) in Christ |
| | 12 | School holidays | | Eph. 3:1–13 | The Mystery Revealed |
| | 19 | | | Eph. 3:14–21 | Power in Action |
| | 26 | School holidays + long weekend | | Eph. 4:1–6 | Unity and Diversity |
| May | 3 | | | Eph. 4:7–16 | The Work of Ministry |
| | 10 | Mother's Day | | Eph. 4:17–5:20 | Holy Living |
| | 17 | | | Eph. 5:21–33 | Wives and Husbands |
| | 24 | Pentecost | | Eph. 6:1–9 | Children, Parents, Workers, Bosses |
| | 31 | | | Eph. 6:10–17 | The Real Fight |
| Jun. | 7 | | | Eph. 6:18–24 | Pray at All Times |
| | 14 | | Exodus 20–23: Life Together | Ex. 20:1–21 | The Constitution |
| | 21 | (Ramadan prayers start Thu 18) | | Ex. 21:1–11 | Human Rights |
| | 28 | | | Ex. 21:12–27 | Against Violence |

| MONTH | DATE | NOTES | SERIES | TEXT | TITLE |
|-------|------|-------|--------|------|-------|
| Jul. | 5 | School holidays | Exodus 20–23: Life Together | Ex. 21:28–22:15 | Property Law |
| | 12 | | | Ex. 22:16–23:9 | Social Responsibilities |
| | 19 | | | Ex. 23:10–19 | National Celebrations |
| | 26 | | John 9–10: Healer, Shepherd, Messiah | John 9:1–12 | Sight for the Blind - Part 1 |
| Aug. | 2 | | | John 9:13–41 | Sight for the Blind - Part 2 |
| | 9 | | | John 10:1–21 | The Good Shepherd |
| | 16 | | | John 10:22–42 | God the Son |
| | 23 | | Psalms: Lord of My Heart | Ps. 139 | Lord of My All |
| | 30 | | | Ps. 13 | Lord of My Sadness |
| Sep. | 6 | Father's Day | | Ps. 37 | Lord of My Anger |
| | 13 | | | Ps. 32 | Lord of My Guilt |
| | 20 | | | Ps. 145 | Lord of My Joy |
| | 27 | School holidays | Ruth: God's People and the World's People | Ruth 1 | Leaving and Cleaving |
| Oct. | 4 | School holidays + long weekend | | Ruth 2 | Laboring and Rewarding |
| | 11 | School holidays | | Ruth 3 | Risking and Honoring |
| | 18 | | | Ruth 4 | Joining and Rejoicing |
| | 25 | | John 11–12: From Death to Life | John 11:1–44 | The Resurrection and the Life |
| Nov. | 1 | | | John 11:45–57 | One for Many |
| | 8 | | | John 12:1–11 | Burial Preparations |
| | 15 | | | John 12:12–19 | The King Has Come |
| | 22 | | | John 12:20–36 | The Fruit of Death |
| | 29 | Advent starts | | John 12:37–50 | Darkness and Light |
| Dec. | 6 | | Exodus 23–31: Preparing for Life in the Land | Ex. 23:20–33 | The Land Promised |
| | 13 | School holidays | | Ex. 24:1–18 | Covenant and Communion |
| | 20 | | | Ex. 25:1–9 | Gifts for Worship |
| | 24 | School holidays/Christmas Eve | | Ex. 25:10–28:43 | Preparing for His Presence |
| | 25 | School holidays/Christmas Day | | Ex. 29:1–46 | The New Priesthood |
| | 26 | School holidays/Christmas Day 2 | | Ex. 30:1–21 | Made for Sacrifice, Atonement, and Cleansing |
| | 27 | School holidays | | Ex. 30:22–38 | The Annointed One |
| Jan. | 3 | School holidays + long weekend | | Ex. 31:1–11 | Creative Gifts |
| | 10 | School holidays | | Ex. 31:12–18 | Reminder to Rest |

PART 3

# PRACTICAL AND PASTORAL CONSIDERATIONS

# 9

# Maximizing Impact

Living in Asia, as one of us does, is an amazing experience as far as food is concerned. The choice of what to eat each day is complicated by an astonishing and sometimes overwhelming mass of culinary delights that can match a variety of wallets and tastes. Food experts say that it is not only taste that matters, but also sight, sound, smell, and even touch. As a result, eating in Asia is a memorable experience because of such things as the bustle and noise of food stalls, the warm humidity of the evenings, the buzzing streetlights, the bustling masses of people, and more besides. All of these combine to make the eating experience even richer than the food, with the result that sometimes it is a simple joy to just stick around after the food has been consumed and enjoy the atmosphere. So while you may be able to order a favorite dish from your local Malaysian take-out restaurant, eating it at home in front of the television is a far cry from eating it on the night streets of Penang. The point is just that there can be a great deal more that contributes to our enjoyment of good food than what is on the plate in front of us.

If we were to follow the Bible's lead in linking the word of God to food (Matt. 4:4; Luke 4:4; cf. Deut. 8:3), then perhaps we might also playfully follow through the analogy above and think about our church services as places where we are serving up the richest food that humans can have—the food of the word of God, which has Christ at its center and therefore can enrich their souls for eternity. If so, then perhaps we could learn from the food experts and make sure that all that we do in our services and our broader church experience makes the food of the word of God delightful and rich. The way to do this is to make sure that we integrate the word of God with all that we do and surround it with things that help our people hear and imbibe it. That is what this chapter is about—maximizing the impact of the word of God.

Not only do we want to avoid the disaster of a famine of the word of God for the people of God, we also believe in and want to make the ministry of the word a rich, well thought-out, and well presented feast for the people of God in our churches so that they might know Christ and enjoy him forever, feed on him in their hearts by faith and thanksgiving, and live lives that glorify him.

## Keeping the Word Central in Scripture

It is not always wise to draw too much from one verse or from a descriptive passage of Scripture. Nevertheless, Acts 2:42 is significant to our thinking in a number of ways and points us in the right direction in terms of getting priorities right in our life together as God's people. There are a few observations that we can make. First, this verse is preceded immediately by one of a number of significant summary statements that are scattered through Acts (2:41, and then 6:7; 9:31; 12:24; 16:5; 19:20), and it therefore comes at a key juncture of the text. Second, it is actually connected to the first summary statement and precedes a number of others, which, like it, focus on early Christian life in Jerusalem (2:42–47; 4:32–37; 5:12–16; 8:1b–4). Third, and most relevant to us, this one stands out for what it tells us in terms of what the early Christians in Jerusalem did when they met together. It records that they devoted themselves to four things: the apostles' teaching, the fellowship, the breaking of bread, and the prayers.

There is some debate as to whether just the first phrase, or the first and second together, are the source of the rest, but it is likely that all flow from the first—that is, from the apostles' teaching. Given that the word for "fellowship" (κοινωνία/*koinonia*) is used only in this location in all of Luke and Acts; that it normally has the sense of "sharing" with or "participating" in something with someone else; and that succeeding descriptions of activity in the early church speak of the common sharing of goods, such sharing is probably what is meant here. The "breaking of bread" probably refers at least to the Lord's Supper, which may have been tied to a common meal as it was associated originally with the Passover feast (as we see in other parts of the New Testament, e.g., Luke 22:7–23; cf. 1 Cor. 11:17–34).

If this analysis is correct, it appears that the first activity—that is, the apostles' teaching—leads to common sharing among the early Christians, participating in a meal together with a focus on the Lord's Supper, and prayers to God. If the apostles' teaching is understood to be hearing God's word through the apostles, the sharing of possessions and meals is directed outward to the community of believers, and prayers go upward to God from the community, then we might present this all diagrammatically in the following way:

Fig. 9.1. The Priority and Centrality of the Word.

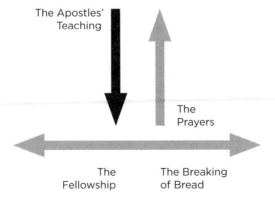

The Apostles' Teaching

The Prayers

The Fellowship

The Breaking of Bread

Such centrality and foundational authority given to God's word is characteristic of the rest of Scripture, with God's revelation climaxing in his speaking through his Son (Heb. 1:1–2), whom we hear about in the gospel. The lesson is that our entire life together as God's people must flow out of his word through the apostles and prophets, with Christ Jesus himself being the cornerstone (Eph. 2:19–22). All we do together must be grounded in God's word in Scripture, which tells us about God's word in his Son.

Once we have observed how so much flows from the priority and centrality of the word, we need to observe how Acts goes on to tell us some of the areas of impact. The believers share lives and support each other, caring for each other and doing what they can to meet each other's needs (4:32–37). They worship and pray together, hearing from each other and supporting new ministries as directed by God through their prophets and teachers (13:1–3). They care for routine needs of the disadvantaged among them (6:1–7) and put elders in place for the teaching, care, and support of the flock (14:19–23). In other words, they do the sorts of things we see discussed and outlined in the New Testament Epistles. Having heard of what God has done in Christ (Romans 1–11), they present their bodies as living sacrifices, holy and acceptable to God, and through their transformation by the renewal of their minds, they discern what the will of God is (12:1–2) and let that affect their lives together as God's people (12:3–15:13).

## Keeping the Word Central through History

It will be helpful for us to give some short historical snapshots of people who worked to keep central things central, particularly the ministry of the word. Our first example is Martin Luther. Between five and six years after Luther nailed his Ninety-Five Theses to the door of the Wittenberg Castle church in 1517, he turned his attention to the reform of worship in his treatise "Concerning the Order of Public Worship." There he railed against the way preaching had been sidelined, such that only reading and singing remained in churches. He therefore set about "to restore it again to its right and proper place."[1] Luther was clear. First, thinking theologically about what happens when God's people meet is critical. Second, God's word has always been at the center of the lives of God's people, and to cut it out from their meeting together is to cut the heart out of Christian gatherings. Third, the right response to our own context and lives, as well as to God both in his word and as a result of his sovereign control over our lives, is to also pray.

Across the sea and slightly later in history, we come to another Reformer, Thomas Cranmer, the archbishop of Canterbury who worked to redesign corporate worship services for the Church of England. The 1662 Book of Common Prayer was the text that gave shape to those services, and it arose from deeply Reformed convictions concerning the centrality and importance of the Scriptures. The impact of those convictions was not only to positively promote the sufficiency of the Scriptures, but also to prohibit non-biblical ideas being taught. Cranmer maintained that of necessity there must be some rules for ordering public worship. However, they should be few in number, plain, and easy to understand. Critical among them is that

> nothing is ordained to be read, but the very pure Word of God, the holy Scriptures, or that which is agreeable to the same; and that in such a Language and Order as is most easy and plain for the understanding both of the Readers and Hearers.[2]

The Book of Common Prayer was intentionally formed by biblical truth and practically focused on the gospel, so it ensured things such as the frequent restating of the gospel and salvation history; biblical theology; daily reading of the Psalms; constant urging

---

1. Martin Luther, "Concerning the Order of Public Worship," in *Martin Luther's Basic Theological Writings*, 3rd ed., ed. William R. Russell and Timothy F. Lull (Minneapolis: Fortress, 2012), 307–9.
2. "Concerning the Service of the Church," in The Book of Common Prayer (Cambridge: Cambridge University Press, n.d.).

from Scripture to turn away from sin, confess it, and turn toward the forgiveness offered in the gospel; and the public reading of Scripture from both Testaments.

A good and reasonably contemporary example of like-minded people from different denominational backgrounds and perspectives grappling with the question of how to keep the Scriptures central in weekly church services can be found in the discussions by D. A. Carson, Mark Ashton, Kent Hughes, and Timothy Keller in the volume *Worship by the Book*, in which they look to define worship and describe how they work to implement their common convictions in their different traditions. In his introductory chapter, "Worship under the Word," Carson interacts with a list of activities described in New Testament churches by Edmund Clowney and observes "how many of the items listed by Clowney are related, in one way or another, to the word."[3] Kent Hughes argues,

> God's word must infuse everything. The careful reading of the word must be central. Hymns and songs must be word-saturated. Prayers must be biblically informed, redolent with biblical reality—often reflecting the very language and structure of Scripture. The preaching of the Word of God must be the Word of God. Such service requires principled, prayerful thought and hard work . . . it must happen in our hearts. Corporate worship must be word-centered if it is to glorify God as it ought.[4]

We see with these small samples from history and contemporary church life that it is important to be deliberate in preventing central things from becoming peripheral, or even totally neglected, in church services. So how then can we work to keep the Scriptures central among all the parts of our weekly corporate gatherings?

---

3. D. A. Carson, "Worship under the Word," in *Worship by the Book*, ed. D. A. Carson (Grand Rapids, MI: Zondervan, 2002), 50.
4. R. Kent Hughes, "Free Church Worship," in *Worship by the Book*, 159.

## Keeping the Word Central in Our Church Services

As we have noted above, and as we all know anyway, there are many things in addition to the preaching of Scripture that are important in the meetings of God's people. It is also good and right that children as well as adults are ministered to, that we sing psalms, hymns, and spiritual songs (Eph. 5:19; Col. 3:16), that we come to God in prayer and intercession (Eph. 6:18 ; 1 Thess. 5:17), that we think about how we care for the disadvantaged in our congregations and beyond (Gal. 2:10), and even that we do other creative things that engage and encourage us. However, as we set ourselves to all of these tasks, we will face the constant tendency that Luther addressed—that is, imitating the medieval church by replacing the word with something else as the focus of our gatherings. It might not be sacramentalism for us, but it might be something like the performance of our music, the quality of our audio-visual presentations, or even our community notices that comes to take priority, with everything else gravitating around it.

So how can we express the centrality of the word but also ensure that it translates to the other aspects of our corporate life? One way is to think about how we can design all of the other parts of our meeting so that they *flow out of* the reading and preaching of the word. If we arrange things this way, it will be impossible not to prioritize the word, even as we give due attention to the rest. We gave two examples of what this might look like when we thought about preaching Psalms 117 and 119 in the last chapter, but it is worth expanding our considerations.

If we were to make our preaching program available to the person responsible for planning our services, he or she would be able to see what the sermon text of the day is, what series it comes from, and, if the planning spreadsheet is expanded, even what the main lessons, emphases, or applications of the sermon will be. Armed with all of this information, the service planner could set about designing a meeting that reinforces, expands, emphasizes, and harmonizes with the text to be preached. This might mean choosing songs that pick up on the sermon's themes or that have the words of the sermon text in their lyrics. It should certainly mean planning the corporate prayers so that they intersect with the sermon's message. It could even mean including more creative or unique elements in the flow of the service that would help the congregation engage more with the Bible passage—performing a short drama, having an extended time of silence, reciting a creed together, and other things.

Of course, it may be that some services need not just thoughtful elements that match the sermon text, but also some that balance it out. If, for example, the passage being preached is very strong on God's judgment, it could be important to set this in context by highlighting God's gracious forgiveness through Jesus in the prayers or songs. Contextual wisdom is always important when planning church services, and a mature theological framework helps the pastor know what needs to be balanced and when. There is a real need for creativity and energy in this work, and it might even be that a church could establish a whole Sunday service planning team whose members can work together, pooling their thinking, bouncing ideas around, and then taking responsibility for the logistics and execution of the services.[5] Not only would this expand the creative potential of the church, it might also create an exciting new area of service for the members that taps into many of their God-given gifts that have formerly lain dormant.

As well as influencing all that is happening within the four walls where the main service is taking place, the preaching program should be integrated into the other ministries that happen at the same time. Fortunately, this should be relatively straightforward for one of the most common ministries that runs in parallel with the church service: the children's program. The leaders of these programs can easily be asked to prepare materials focusing

---

5. A volume that discusses how to creatively make the most of the Sunday service is Nancy Beach, *An Hour On Sunday: Creating Moments of Transformation and Wonder* (Grand Rapids, MI: Zondervan, 2004).

on the same text as the sermon. As well as offering children the whole Bible, the beauty of this approach is that it means children and their parents or caregivers will have the same parts of Scripture in their heads after church each Sunday. This can be a great aid to conversations about the Bible at home and to parents being more closely engaged with their children's spiritual development (which, after all, is primarily their responsibility). The family can all learn and grow in parallel.

To be sure, there are some cases in which this approach can bring extra challenges, as there are parts of the Bible that we might feel uncomfortable sharing with children. Do we teach them about the violence that is found in many Old Testament narratives? What about the parts of Scripture that deal with sex? Our impulse might be to edit these out—as most children's Bibles do—but it is probably better that we work hard to come up with age-appropriate ways of helping our children learn about them. It may be that some of the violence we read about can be properly spoken of as fair punishment—something that makes sense to children. And we might talk about sex as the special love that should be reserved for married people. The great risk of editing the children's program based only on our gut sense for what will trouble our kids is the same as the risk in editing the adult program: we provide a filtered, thinned-down version of God's revelation to his people. And if our impulse is to withhold texts that include such elements as exposed bodies and death, we could end up quietly bypassing Jesus's crucifixion—as some children's Bibles do—and so losing one of the most important and integrating stories in the whole Bible.

### The Public Reading of Scripture

One part of the service that deserves particular comment is the up-front reading of the Bible. Imagine the situation. We've made sure that the ministry of the word is central and the meeting has been planned meticulously. In the middle of the meeting, the reader of our Bible passage steps up to the lectern. The microphone crackles while he fiddles with it. He begins to read with a deadly serious look on his face. His bespectacled eyes set themselves firmly on the small print of his personal Bible, which is different from the version both in the pews and on the data projector screen. He begins to read the long but exciting text of 1 Samuel 17, concerning David and Goliath. The reading is monotone, dull, sonorous. Eventually he announces the end and sits down, to the relief of those who are still trying to keep awake and keep their eyes on their own Bibles. Your planning has been scuttled at the last possible moment by poor execution of one of the key things the Bible has urged you not to neglect: the public reading of Scripture (1 Tim. 4:13).

Do not let this happen. There are probably three options if you find that the Bible is being read poorly in your church. The first is to invest in training the readers to do a better job. This might including having them learn the pronunciation of any difficult people or place names and practice the pacing and cadence of the reading. Even noticing where the commas are in the passage can make a big difference. Training readers might also involve helping them know how to project their voices or use a microphone so that it doesn't boom or ping. The second option might be to take some of the readers off the roster. If they are not gifted in public reading and cannot be trained, they might need to realize that they have misunderstood the gifts that God has given them. The exciting thing about this is that they then have a fresh chance to investigate what their real gifts of service might be. Finally, the preacher can do the reading himself. In some countries of the world, this is the default option, and there is a lot of sense in it. The preacher has hopefully spent most of the week in the text. He is excited about it and its message, and he knows where it needs emphasis or change of speed. However, having said this, it is true that there are some fine preachers who cannot read well in public (their preaching is not from a full manuscript). Hopefully they are aware of any weakness in this area and allow others who are better equipped to do the reading.

## Integrating Other Church Ministries with Preaching

We always do well to remember that as important as our regular corporate gatherings are, "church" means far more than just a weekly event. The local church is the people of God who live out the gospel together not only on Sundays, but through the whole week. In many cases, this happens organically through the countless casual and spontaneous interactions that church members have with each other and the world each day. Meals and care packages are dropped off at neighbors' homes. Children are brought devotional books for their birthdays. Long conversations about doubts happen over cups of coffee at the local cafe. Prayers are offered at the school gate for a young mom going through a hard time. Teenagers gift each other new worship music over the internet. Members talk to their friends about child sponsorship and sacrificial support for missionaries. Workers tell their colleagues about how faith in Jesus makes more sense than any other way of life. This is all fantastic and to be greatly encouraged.

But in addition to all of this unstructured gospel living, many church communities also oversee more formal midweek activities too. These vary from place to place, but might include things such as small Bible study groups in people's homes, evening youth groups, community care and engagement programs, and annual retreats. Just as it is possible to align the weekly sermon text with all that happens on Sunday, churches can also shape their formal non-Sunday activities around the preaching passage too, furthering the focus and integrated approach to sitting under the word and reducing the scattershot approach to growing the body of Christ.

Bible study groups are probably the easiest activity to marry to the preaching program—they can simply study the sermon text each week. There are a number of great benefits to this approach. One of the main benefits is that the members of the small group get to spend more time in the same text of Scripture, which enables them to dig deeper into its meaning and message for them. Also, the group leaders can get some guidance from the pastor about the passage before they lead their studies, and they can bring questions to him, knowing that he has recently spent a lot of time studying it in preparation for preaching. Finally, when all of a local church's small groups study the preaching passage during the week, the whole church can grow together. Too often we think about our spiritual growth as individuals, and there are certainly particular ways that each Christian needs to grow that may be different from those around them. But each local church also needs to be continually growing as a faith *community*. This involves jointly repenting of our corporate sins and working properly together so that the body may be built up in love (Eph. 4:11–16). While it is possible for the body to grow as different members sit under different parts of the Scriptures—and indeed, this is always the case as different members read the Bible in all kinds of different contexts—there can be something powerful about the whole body sitting under the same texts together. Of course, aligning our Bible study groups just further reinforces the unity we have as we all sit under the same text being preached on Sundays.

However, the group needs to know if the pastor prefers for them to study the passage before or after the Sunday when the sermon is preached, as this affects the type of study that they do, and perhaps the type of sermon that should be preached too. If the study comes first, it will raise a lot of questions that group members will hope the pastor will answer in the sermon. However, if the sermon comes first, the group can helpfully come together with a reasonable understanding of the passage and can then spend more of their time considering its application in their particular circumstances. Both approaches can work well; there just needs to be clarity about which is being taken.

Tying community outreach to the preaching program can be very powerful too. Many churches do this well at Christmas and Easter. They might prepare special invitations to church services for those occasions, then deploy their door-knocking teams to take them through the neighborhood or ask their office teams to push them out on social media. They might have not just formal church services at these times either, but also take the opportunity to deliver Easter eggs to hospitals or hot cross buns to university students, each tagged with seasonal Bible verses. They might go Christmas caroling in nursing homes or prepare festive meals for homeless shelters, distributing copies of the New Testament at the same time. These are all great ways to make the most of the season, and all those who turn up at church will hear a message being proclaimed that neatly matches what they have experienced outside. The challenge is to take this Christmas and Easter thinking to the entirety of our churches' outreach programs. What invitations could we extend to our neighborhoods as we prepare for our short preaching series on Nahum? How could we share Christ's love and Christ's challenge at our local shopping centers in ways that tie in with our sermons on 1 John? Once again, we need creativity to do this well, but it can actually be a lot of fun.

Once, one of us was preaching through a section of John's Gospel and came to chapter 13, where Jesus washes the disciples' feet before the Last Supper. As an outreach activity, the church set up a stall at the local community farmers market, laid out a huge sheet of canvas, and invited people to take their shoes off and walk across it after stepping in some tubs of mud that we had dyed with food coloring. Lots of people gave this a try and thought it was good fun. (One engaged couple from the church led the way by doing a sort of muddy bridal waltz up and down the canvas.) Not only did this activity allow us to present the church as a group that knew how to enjoy life (something that is not always believed about the church), but it also seeded some good questions. How would people get their feet clean? Why this activity? We were able to use the day as a chance to invite people to our next Sunday service, and anyone who came heard John 13:1–20 preached and saw the canvas hanging up at the front of the church, covered in muddy footprints. Later, we took the canvas down and cut it into small squares for anyone who wanted to take a piece of the community art home. There was something very helpful about tying our outreach to our regular preaching program, and both were enhanced by the synergy.

Church retreats offer different opportunities to deepen the congregation's engagement with the word. Retreats serve many purposes, but two of the most important are that they give members of the church substantially greater opportunities to invest in their relationships with one another and to soak in a bigger package of teaching than is possible on Sundays. A retreat could be used to deliver a complete seriatim expository sermon series on a short book of the Bible or one whole section of a longer book. This may be one of the most effective ways to help a congregation really come to know a book; it is easy to imagine people coming off a retreat feeling like they really understand 2 Kings 1–10 or Titus after having had their heads there for three days. Another possibility is to make retreats the times for topical or doctrinal series. We have already argued that most preaching in church should be exposition, and yet there are good reasons to do some topical teaching. If church retreats are used for this purpose, there is good time available to sink into complex theological subjects without detracting from, or derailing, the overall plan to preach through the whole Bible in thirty-five years. Of course, topical preaching must be well planned and prepared for too. The choice and cycle of topics is very important, as is the need for careful preparation that results in balanced talks. Whatever a church decides to do, it would be a great shame to squander the opportunity presented by retreats for extensive corporate teaching. And a retreat that is planned with a good sense for the church's place in its preaching program is even more beneficial to the members.

One very practical way to facilitate good integration of the preaching program with the other ministries of the church, be they Sunday or midweek activities, is to produce a booklet or web space for each preaching series. This could include an extract from the preaching calendar showing all of the sermon texts and titles, as well as useful background information on the book or book section being studied. There might be extra notes for Bible study groups, children's programs, or other ministries of the church. A preacher should be able to develop resources such as this quite easily given all of the work that he is already doing to prepare the sermon series; he might even decide that drafting these booklets is a standard goal for his initial preparation time on each series.

Having produced this booklet, the preacher can share it with the leaders of all of the church's other ministries as part of their briefing on the upcoming teaching. We would even recommend that the church schedule these leaders' briefings a few weeks out from the start of each new sermon series to give the leaders plenty of time to prepare their material—and to help the pastor get into good rhythms of preparing early. A different version of the booklet could even be produced for the members of the congregation, and it might include spaces for them to take notes from the sermons or Bible studies. Whether or not it is used this way, a tangible resource like this can be a great help in immersing each member of the church in each preaching series.

## A Brief Note on Branding and Marketing

For some people, the whole notion of a church branding its programs and then marketing them to the world smacks of everything we should oppose: commodifying the faith, seeing people as consumers, entering into competition for attendees with other churches, and so on. All of this leaves a very bad taste in our mouths.

Certainly where church leaders do adopt commercial philosophies as well as business tools, or where the church's image becomes more important than its message, there is a great deal to fear. But it is quite possible to make good and holy use of that which is so often used for godless purposes. Just as a church can use electric guitars, data projectors, office software packages, passcodes for secure areas, online banking services, and industrial ovens, so too it can use design and promotion that is more commonly associated with other settings. If the ultimate goal is to bring people to Christ and assist them in engaging with him through his word, we should feel free to make use of whatever will make that possible.

The value of branding and marketing for outsiders is obvious: it lets them know what is happening at church and that they would be most welcome to visit. And if we uniquely brand each sermon series, we might find that we create a variety of points of connection with different people. Calling a series on Exodus 20–23 "Living Well Together" might catch the interest of someone who is particularly community minded. A series on the book of Joel called "Returning to God" might connect with a dechurched person who is feeling convicted about having strayed. A series on John 13–14 that was simply called "The Last Supper" and used graphics based on the famous Leonardo da Vinci painting might appeal to someone who has a sense for classical Christianity but does not know much of its substance. Of course, it is hard to predict what will and will not work, but it is better to at least be thinking about these kinds of connections than not making any effort at all. Even if the series branding does not end up doing much for outsiders, it will be another way of integrating the overall experience of the members and promoting the centrality of the word of God in the life of the church.

The quality question looms large over any discussion of branding and marketing. The reality nowadays is that poor-quality print and digital media not only fails to engage people, but actually puts them off. The message that is sent by a church that uses clip art, kitschy graphics, or ugly designs is that it does not care about the things on the page. We might say that what matters is the content, not the presentation, and that it is superficial to be turned off by tacky design, but no one actually believes this. Think about a wedding invitation. Usually it comes on a nice card with a beautiful design, and the reason for this is that the bride and groom want the medium to reflect the importance of the event. To be sure, they could invite you to their wedding by scrawling the time and place on the back of a dirty paper napkin, but that would not make you feel like someone they are very eager to have with them on the big day, and it might make you think that they are not even all that interested in getting married. The message is inseparable from the medium, so it is worth putting in the effort to design things well so that the people who see them feel that you value them and the word of God. The overall effort that a church puts into its presentation says something to the world, and that is equally true whether we are talking about our media or our attention to cleaning the carpet, kitchen, and toilets.

10

# Practical Implications
# and Realities

If you have been working in pastoral ministry for any length
of time, you may be thinking that the model of preaching we
are proposing—and the idea of structuring a church around its
preaching calendar—is all well and good in theory, but real life
in a local church is so messy and unpredictable that it could not
possibly be so neatly ordered and systematized. We would agree
with the sentiment, and perhaps go even further to say that local
churches *ought* to be somewhat messy and unpredictable, as
they should be places where people are able to let their guard
down, bring all their struggles and failings, share their concerns,
and feel genuinely welcomed, loved, and accepted even when
everything in their lives is falling apart. If we have a church culture where the unspoken expectation is that everyone should be
living a picture-perfect life and that church is a place where we
showcase our magnificent ability to always be in control and to
cope graciously with whatever life throws at us, we are doing
our congregations a great disservice and potentially setting them
up for a terrible fall. The only church that is full of such people
is a dishonest one that is likely to be very resistant to having its

true sinfulness, weakness, and fear exposed to the healing balm of the word and Spirit.

However, as much as we believe all of this, we do not think it follows that structured preaching and church programs are ineffective, impossible, or counterproductive. On the contrary, the fact that churches are full of broken people living messy lives only underscores the importance of the weekly gatherings being safe and dependable rather than another experience of chaos and disorder. We must work hard to implement our convictions in stable and practically workable systems, accounting for all the complexities of life in the real world. This does not mean that we cannot be flexible when flexibility is required, but simply that our flexibility must be within a well-executed operation.

## Theologically Aligned and Well Coordinated Preachers

As we plan to lead our churches from the pulpit, one of the first things we must do is ensure that everyone on our preaching team is on the same page. At its most basic, this means that we must all share common theological convictions. It is disastrous for the associate pastor to step up to give a sermon or a sermon series that contradicts the senior pastor's teaching. Some churches may feel that this is healthy, as it shows the congregation that there are some things in Scripture that are not completely cut-and-dried and on which different interpreters have different views. There is truth in this, but the practical reality in a local church is that such disagreement can leave many in the congregation in a place where we do not want them to be. They might come to think that it does not matter whether what we believe is actually true, so long as we have some justification for believing it. This is the path to theological relativism and it might lead some to develop itching ears that seek out preachers who teach the Scriptures in ways that they like rather than in ways that are true. Of course, if they do this, they will be also ignoring the pastoral leadership of their home church.

Others might come to think that the Bible is so ambiguous that they must take all preaching with a pinch of salt, and they might subconsciously begin to believe that we cannot truly know much about God through his word. There is something humble and healthy about admitting our own ignorance and incompetence to understand things, but when this leads us to treat the word of God like shifting sand instead of solid rock, we have gone too far. Preachers should never claim infallibility, but neither should they foster an environment in which they undercut confidence in the faithful interpretation of the Scriptures. A wise balance is needed at this point, and broad theological agreement among preachers is an important part of setting the right tone.

Usually, members of a preaching team are not in any strong disagreement with one another. Most churches have appointment processes that ensure agreement to a common doctrinal position, and it is unlikely that many associate pastors would want to work with a senior pastor whose theological views they reject. Problems more commonly arise in the finer details of the interpretation of particular texts. Once, in one of our churches, the preaching team agreed to share the preaching of the book of Ecclesiastes. This caused some problems when the second preacher offered a slightly alternative understanding of the Hebrew word *hebel* (הֶבֶל, "warm breath" or "vapor," often translated as "futility" or "vanity") to that of the first. Given that so much of Ecclesiastes rests on what we think this word means, the congregation was given two different understandings of the whole book. This could have been avoided if the members of the preaching team had interacted more during their preparation and even had a robust theological conversation about the meaning of *hebel* before tackling the series. There could be myriad other examples of situations in which the whole church would be well served by the preaching team taking the time to resolve these sorts of issues. Without entering here into the details of church leadership, we would say that where there is an issue that cannot be resolved before the sermons are to be preached, the senior pastor, as the church's lead teacher and chief undershepherd, should have the final say in what is communicated from the pulpit.

Things are more complicated when it comes to visiting preachers who are not a part of the church's regular ministry team. The senior pastor must take responsibility for ensuring that any guest's theological position is orthodox, and this might require him to be proactive in many cases. This might mean asking a guest preacher to assent to a doctrinal statement. It could mean taking the time to listen to a number of a guest preacher's sermon recordings or to read things he has written. Or it might require the senior pastor to catch up with him over coffee to ask some theological questions. This might sound a bit awkward, and we might fear offending our guests, but if our priority is maintaining the doctrinal standards of our churches, we ought to be happy to do this, and our guests should appreciate our care for the flock.

Having established the baseline like this, we then need to ask how our guests fit into our preaching calendar. Commonly, itinerant preachers arrive with a few set-piece sermons on offer. These are often very good, as they have been honed and polished over the years, and so we can be tempted to let guests preach texts of their choosing. But, of course, to do so would be to prioritize their convenience over our congregation's planned diet of Scripture—it almost seems to be putting the cart before the horse. It is far better to ask guests to preach things that fit in with the church's program. They might need more lead time for their preparation, and some might even choose not to come if their freedom is curtailed in this way. But in the end, we will have peace with this knowing that it really would not be appropriate for occasional visitors to set the preaching program of our churches.

## Disruptions to the Program

As much as we would love it if our churches always ran like clockwork, they never do. Sometimes, a congregation is rocked by a significant event that demands a response, and sometimes that response means that we need to change our best-laid plans. These types of events might be internal to the church: perhaps one of our young people is involved in a serious car accident, one of our leaders is caught in an extramarital affair, or one of our Bible study groups openly challenges the pastor's authority. We do not much like to think about these sorts of things, as they are the worst parts of church life, but, sadly, in a fallen world, they do happen from time to time. Only naive church leaders would think that they could altogether avoid such situations as they tend the people of God.

Some big events might be external to the congregation. These could include a natural disaster, such as a wildfire or flood in the local area; a controversial piece of legislation passing into law; or even something as monumental as the coordinated terrorist attacks of September 11, 2001, in the United States. Ideally, a pastor's seminary training should have prepared him not only to speak biblical truth into these situations, but also to minister among the people with biblically based tools for crisis care, administration of discipline, and conflict resolution. He should also have been given ample opportunities to reflect on his strengths and weaknesses when dealing with tense and intense situations so that he does not lose his nerve or composure under pressure, but is able to engage with the right mixture of pathos and gospel-grounded strength.

But what happens to the preaching program at times like these? One possibility could be not to change anything and to continue with the program as set. In some circumstances, there could be a brilliant wisdom in this. It might send the message that it is the word of God, rather than the issue of the moment, that continues to set the agenda for the church, and there might be times when that is a very important thing for people to know. It could also be that this approach would relativize an issue that one part of the church is feeling intensely, but that the preacher feels should not dominate the entire life of the community.

The obvious risk of persevering on the same track, however, is that the pastoral care of the congregation could become divorced from the preaching, as though there were two different spheres to church life—the up-front official and the behind-the-scenes personal—that do not really overlap. If the issue is large enough and this disjunct is too strong, even the best expository sermon will fail to connect with the congregation; the people will be completely distracted by the elephant in the room and might wonder why their pastor is not guiding them through the dominating problem.

One alternative, then, is to put the preaching program on hold and to address the issue from the pulpit, drawing on the appropriate biblical texts. Other approaches might include organizing a special church meeting, writing a letter to all members of the church, or preparing a theological and pastoral reflection for publication on the website. As is so often the case, there is no fixed right or wrong in these situations. Instead, leaders need to make their decisions based on prayerful, reflective, pastoral wisdom.

If the choice is to diverge from the preaching program, one of the implications is that the program might then need to be reworked to account for the missed sermon or sermons. In some cases, this might be straightforward; perhaps the disruption is only for one week, and the current series is to be followed by a one-off sermon on a psalm. In that case, all that would need to happen is to bump the rest of the series by a week and drop the psalm for the time being. In other cases, things might be far more complicated and require a significant overhaul of the plan for months to come. One way of minimizing the disruption might be to preach the missing sermons to audio or video, posting them online and then encouraging the church members to listen to them. Perhaps it would be appropriate for midweek Bible study group leaders to be asked to change their programs so that their groups could listen together at their normal meeting times. Whatever is worked out, we would encourage coming up with a solution that does not result in some parts of Scripture simply being cut from the church's teaching schedule altogether.

If that happens, there is a low likelihood of those texts ever being preached, and certainly not as part of a coherent series.

## Tracking

Discussing the occasional need to adjust the preaching program takes us back to our planning spreadsheet and another practical aspect of managing our big preaching project. As we are continually planning our preaching programs, we also need to be accounting for what we have already preached. It would be impossible for anyone to keep the details of a multiyear preaching program in his head, especially when that program is building to cover thirty-five years. Therefore, we require a good system of logging, or tracking, the sermons we have preached.

Good record keeping is an essential part of any well-run enterprise, as nobody wants to have to trawl through disorganized piles of files (either hard copy or electronic) to get accurate data about the work he has been doing. Worse than this is trawling through such piles only to find that the data has gone missing or was never recorded in the first place. So when we are deciding if we should preach through a major section of Isaiah sometime in the next twelve months, we obviously need to know how far we went the last time we preached from the book. But more than this, we also want to have a sense for how much of the Latter Prophets the congregation has heard in the last twelve or twenty-four months, and even how much they will have heard by this time next year if we go ahead with our Isaiah series.

It is very easy to do all of our tracking in the same computer file that we use for planning. All that is needed is some way of distinguishing between sermons that have been preached in the past and sermons that are to be preached in the future. Then, one set of tallies and graphs can be prepared from the fixed, but weekly growing, data of the past, and another set from the live and changeable data of the projected future program. The below example of our expanded file shows what this could look like.

Fig. 10.1. Annual Preaching Calendar (with Past and Future Sermons).

| MONTH | DATE | NOTES | SERIES | TEXT | TITLE | CORPA* | PREACHER |
|---|---|---|---|---|---|---|---|
| Jan. | 4 | | Joel: Returning to God | Joel 1:1–2:17 | Sin's Price & Pain | LP | Associate |
| | 11 | School holidays | | Joel 2:18–27 | Healing & Wholeness | LP | Associate |
| | 18 | | | Joel 2:28–3:17 | The Day of the Lord | LP | Associate |
| | 25 | School holidays + long weekend | | Joel 3:18–21 | Hope for God's People | LP | Associate |
| Feb. | 1 | | John 7–8: Jesus in Public | John 7:1–24 | Meeting Expectations? | G | Lead Pastor |
| | 8 | | | John 7:25–36 | Knowing God, Going to God | G | Lead Pastor |
| | 15 | Lent starts Wed 18 | | John 7:37–52 | Search and You Will See | G | Lead Pastor |
| | 22 | | | John 8:12–20 | God on His Side | G | Lead Pastor |
| Mar. | 1 | | | John 8:21–30 | Two Ways to Die | G | Lead Pastor |
| | 8 | Public holiday long weekend | | John 8:31–38 | The Truth Will Set You Free | G | Lead Pastor |
| | 15 | | | John 8:39–59 | Deadly Relationships | G | Lead Pastor |
| | 22 | | Ephesians: One in Christ | Eph. 1:1–14 | Every Spiritual Blessing | AE | Lead Pastor |
| TODAY | 29 | Palm Sunday | | Eph. 1:15–23 | Called into Hope | AE | Lead Pastor |
| Apr. | 2 | Maundy Thursday | | | *No sermon* | | |
| | 3 | Good Friday | | Eph. 2:1–10 | Saved by Grace | AE | Lead Pastor |
| | 5 | Easter Day (End Daylight Saving) | | Eph. 2:11–22 | One (Temple?) in Christ | AE | Lead Pastor |
| | 12 | School holidays | | Eph. 3:1–13 | The Mystery Revealed | AE | Lead Pastor |
| | 19 | | | Eph. 3:14–21 | Power in Action | AE | Lead Pastor |
| | 26 | School holidays + long weekend | | Eph. 4:1–6 | Unity and Diversity | AE | Lead Pastor |
| May | 3 | | | Eph. 4:7–16 | The Work of Ministry | AE | Lead Pastor |
| | 10 | Mother's Day | | Eph. 4:17–5:20 | Holy Living | AE | Lead Pastor |
| | 17 | | | Eph. 5:21–33 | Wives and Husbands | AE | Lead Pastor |
| | 24 | Pentecost | | Eph. 6:1–9 | Children, Parents, Workers, Bosses | AE | Lead Pastor |
| | 31 | | | Eph. 6:10–17 | The Real Fight | AE | Lead Pastor |
| Jun. | 7 | | | Eph. 6:18–24 | Pray at All Times | AE | Lead Pastor |
| | 14 | | Exodus 20–23: Life Together | Ex. 20:1–21 | The Constitution | T | Lead Pastor |
| | 21 | (Ramadan prayers start Thu 18) | | Ex. 21:1–11 | Human Rights | T | Associate |
| | 28 | | | Ex. 21:12–27 | Against Violence | T | Associate |

*T = Torah; LP = Latter Prophets; W = Writings; G = Gospels; AE = Acts & Epistles

| MONTH | DATE | NOTES | SERIES | TEXT | TITLE | CORPA | PREACHER |
|---|---|---|---|---|---|---|---|
| Jul | 5 | | | Ex. 21:28–22:15 | Property Law | T | Associate |
| | 12 | School holidays | Exodus 20–23: Life Together | Ex. 22:16–23:9 | Social Responsibilities | T | Lead Pastor |
| | 19 | | | Ex. 23:10–19 | National Celebrations | T | Lead Pastor |
| | 26 | | | John 9:1–12 | Sight for the Blind - Part 1 | G | Lead Pastor |
| Aug | 2 | | John 9–10: Healer, Shepherd, Messiah | John 9:13–41 | Sight for the Blind - Part 2 | G | Lead Pastor |
| | 9 | | | John 10:1–21 | The Good Shepherd | G | Lead Pastor |
| | 16 | | | John 10:22–42 | God the Son | G | Guest |
| | 23 | | | Ps. 139 | Lord of My All | W | Associate |
| | 30 | | | Ps. 13 | Lord of My Sadness | W | Associate |
| Sep | 6 | Father's Day | Psalms: Lord of My Heart | Ps. 37 | Lord of My Anger | W | Associate |
| | 13 | | | Ps. 32 | Lord of My Guilt | W | Associate |
| | 20 | | | Ps. 145 | Lord of My Joy | W | Associate |
| | 27 | School holidays | | Ruth 1 | Leaving and Cleaving | W | Lead Pastor |
| Oct | 4 | School holidays + long weekend | Ruth: God's People and the World's People | Ruth 2 | Laboring and Rewarding | W | Lead Pastor |
| | 11 | School holidays | | Ruth 3 | Risking and Honoring | W | Lead Pastor |
| | 18 | | | Ruth 4 | Joining and Rejoicing | W | Lead Pastor |
| | 25 | | | John 11:1–44 | The Resurrection and the Life | G | Lead Pastor |
| Nov | 1 | | | John 11:45–57 | One for Many | G | Lead Pastor |
| | 8 | | John 11–12: From Death to Life | John 12:1–11 | Burial Preparations | G | Lead Pastor |
| | 15 | | | John 12:12–19 | The King Has Come | G | Lead Pastor |
| | 22 | | | John 12:20–36 | The Fruit of Death | G | Lead Pastor |
| | 29 | Advent starts | | John 12:37–50 | Darkness and Light | G | Lead Pastor |
| Dec | 6 | | | Ex. 23:20–33 | The Land Promised | T | Lead Pastor |
| | 13 | School holidays | | Ex. 24:1–18 | Covenant and Communion | T | Lead Pastor |
| | 20 | | | Ex. 25:1–9 | Gifts for Worship | T | Lead Pastor |
| | 24 | School holidays/Christmas Eve | Exodus 23–31: Preparing for Life in the Land | Ex. 25:10–28:43 | Preparing for His Presence | T | Lead Pastor |
| | 25 | School holidays/Christmas Day | | Ex. 29:1–46 | The New Priesthood | T | Lead Pastor |
| | 26 | School holidays/Christmas Day 2 | | Ex. 30:1–21 | Made for Sacrifice, Atonement, and Cleansing | T | Lead Pastor |
| | 27 | School holidays | | Ex. 30:22–38 | The Annointed One | T | Lead Pastor |
| Jan | 3 | School holidays + long weekend | | Ex. 31:1–11 | Creative Gifts | T | Guest |
| | 10 | School holidays | | Ex. 31:12–18 | Reminder to Rest | T | Guest |

Fig. 10.2. Data on Preaching and Preachers.

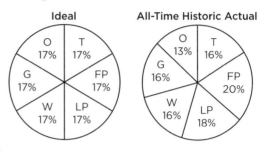

**SCRIPTURE SECTIONS**

T = Torah
FP = Former Prophets
LP = Latter Prophets
W = Writings
G = Gospels
O = Other NT

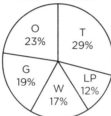

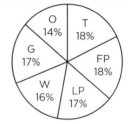

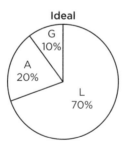

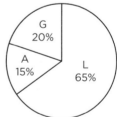

**PREACHERS**

L = Lead Pastor
A = Associate
G = Guest

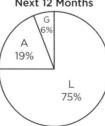

These are not the only graphs that could be made, but they give a sense for what can be done. Having each graph linked to the preaching program means that we can quickly see the impact of different future program proposals as we make various changes. In the example above, we can see that our proposed program for the next twelve months is very heavy on New Testament compared to our ideal, and that the Former and Latter Prophets are most poorly represented—the Former Prophets not being preached at all. But when we look at the impact of this proposed program on our overall historic balance, we find that it does not skew us away from our ideal, but actually brings us a little closer to it. This is because in the past, we preached a great number of sermons from the Former Prophets and a relatively small number from the Gospels. Therefore, this upcoming program offers a helpful corrective.

Our graphs also quickly show us that over the next year we will be reasonably close to our ideal in terms of sharing the preaching load. The lead pastor will rightly take the lion's share of the responsibility to feed the flock, the associate will have many opportunities to relieve the lead and develop his own preaching, and guests will be called on only sparingly. The lead pastor, in fact, will be preaching a little more than the notional ideal in the coming twelve months, and this is a deliberate choice to help make up for excessive dependence on guest preachers in the past. Even after the projected period has passed, guest preachers will still be overrepresented in the historical preaching program.

There are no doubt many further ways that this preaching calendar could be utilized to help the preaching team shape a thoughtful program of teaching. While it is simple, it is a powerful tool that helps us translate ideas into reality and allows us to do top-level evaluations of the preaching and teaching plan at a glance. Once a system like this is set up, the preaching team might be surprised at how constantly they use it for reference and to help guide their planning.

A good tracking system not only helps an individual preacher or the current preaching team, but it might be of immeasurable intergenerational value to the church. If the time comes for the preacher to move on, his successor will greatly appreciate being able to look over the congregation's historical diet of Scripture. In most cases, a new pastor will arrive eager to preach a strong first series of sermons. But if he finds that the book he would naturally preach from first was preached only six months ago, he might be wise to reconsider his choice. Similarly, as he plans, he will do well to account for all the preaching the congregation has already sat under and to seek out those parts of the whole counsel of God that have not yet been communicated.

An older Christian gentleman once reflected that he knew that whenever a new junior associate pastor joined his church's preaching team, the church would be in for another series on Mark's Gospel because Mark was a focus text at the seminary from which most of the church's appointments graduated. No doubt each new associate appreciated being able to kick off his preaching career in a book that he knew well, but this might not have been the best way to continually feed and grow the established members of the congregation. If the church had kept good preaching records, the preachers would have been able to set different debut series for their new associates, even if that pushed the associates beyond their comfort zones.

It is worth saying that in keeping a record like this, it is always good to collect more data than you immediately have need for, just in case it might come in handy in the years or decades ahead. It takes only a brief moment to fill in a couple of extra fields in a spreadsheet, but that might save hours of work if the day comes when you want to analyze that information.

# 11

# Personal Implications
# for the Preacher

In an earlier chapter, we observed that the believers in the early church devoted themselves to the apostles' teaching, the fellowship, the breaking of bread, and the prayers (Acts 2:42). We saw how all that we do when we meet together as God's people flows from God's word about his Son and his purposes in his Son. Since this is so, pastors of God's people should be focused on the same priorities and should not be overwhelmed by the inevitable, necessary, and even important other aspects of our ministry. A sprint through the Pastoral Epistles will make this emphasis clear, as will an examination of most of the epistolary works in the New Testament (just think of Romans or Ephesians as examples).

Focusing on Paul's first epistle to Timothy, we observe the apostle opening by exhorting Timothy to "charge certain persons not to teach any different doctrine"—that is, to make sure that what is central is "sound doctrine" and those things that are "in accordance with the gospel of the glory of the blessed God" (1 Tim. 1:3, 10–11). He is to ensure that proper order is maintained in congregational life and that the teaching of God's people is properly exercised by the right people (1 Tim. 2:8–15). Paul reminds Timothy of the truths that undergird godly living (3:16) before going on to warn him that false teaching constantly threatens to lead people away from the truth (4:1–3), that good things are made holy by the word of God and prayer (vv. 4–5), and that Timothy, as a "good servant of Christ Jesus," will be "trained in the words of the faith and of the good doctrine" that he has inherited and been taught (v. 6). He is to "command and teach" (v. 11) trustworthy truths, such as those of verse 10, to set believers an example "in speech, in conduct, in love, in faith, in purity" (v. 12), and to devote himself to "the public reading of Scripture, to exhortation, to teaching," not neglecting the gift given to him but keeping a close watch on himself and his teaching (vv. 13–16).

This brief survey of the first four chapters of 1 Timothy indicates a clear focus for the pastors of the Lord's people—knowing and grounding people in the truths of Scripture in such a way that those truths feed down into their daily lives. In the rest of the Pastoral Epistles, Paul also urges Timothy and Titus to appoint others who will do the same.

### Engaging in Ongoing, Humble, In-Depth Bible Study

The godly pastor of God's people is therefore a person who is constantly growing in his love for and grasp of biblical truth. More so than others, the pastor is to spend time in the Scriptures, not just to teach others but also to inform his own life and ministry.

One of the great joys of a systematic, expository preaching ministry that is done well is that of being in the Scriptures for a significant amount of time each week, grappling with the text in depth, reading what others have thought, but also thinking about how the original context and meaning of the text in its own context intersects with your congregation and their needs. However, if you are going to do the sorts of things that we have suggested in this book, then you need to do more than sermon preparation. To preach the breadth of the Bible, you need to be an *ongoing student of the Bible.* You cannot rely only on what you learned in college or in the last good book that you read.

The critical thing in all of this is to read the Bible for yourself. The need is for a rigorous and widespread personal Bible-reading program that is separate from your preparation for the sermon. Such reading enriches your knowledge and understanding of Scripture, and helps you integrate that knowledge with your ministry of the word. It also enriches your biblical, systematic, and gospel theology, and enables you to adequately and intelligently critique the commentators that you read. This especially requires that you be growing in understanding of those parts of the Bible that you do not currently know so well. For example, perhaps you have never really spent much time in 1 and 2 Chronicles, and you know that you do not really have a good sense for what those books are about. If you never plan to preach these books, you may feel that studying them is unnecessary. However, if you plan to preach the whole Bible, they will become unavoidable, as will other books that are often neglected, such as Leviticus, Song of Solomon, Ecclesiastes, 2 Peter, or Revelation.

What we are saying is that the real challenge is to commit to engaging with more of the Bible. This is not just so that you will have a greater volume of learning, but also because you need to be a model of what is required of all God's people—that is, to be ready to hear things from God that you may not have heard before. He might have confronting lessons, or even discipline, for you in these understudied texts to which you need to pay attention. Placing yourself under the whole counsel of God will make it less likely that you can hide from anything that God wants to speak into your life as you perhaps could if your ministry focused only on a subsection of the Bible. In the end, this is no more than you are asking of your congregation, and so it is entirely appropriate for a preacher to lead the way in submitting himself to every part of Scripture. With this having been said, each person must develop what works best for him in this area. Whatever shape this takes, we recommend widespread, daily, consecutive reading from both Testaments, perhaps linked with seriatim and repetitive reading through the Psalms. This should be a minimum. Within this larger plan, you could also separate your reading in the New Testament into reading in two sections: the Gospels and Acts/Epistles. If your grasp of original languages is good, you might even read a few verses each day of at least your strongest language.

As far as sermon preparation is concerned, it is also very important that the preacher of God's word reads and analyzes that word for himself *before* turning to the commentators for their interpretations. There are all sorts of reasons for this. For example, while commentators are unpacking a text, they are also interacting with other commentators about issues that are often not at the core of the passage. They are often not asking or answering the questions that ordinary people in the pews have. This means that they often feed upon and depend upon each other rather than having your congregation or their questions in mind. So it is more helpful for you to interact first with the text yourself without the commentators' agendas, and also with your congregation in mind. This will help you when you finally read the commentators. You will ask them the right questions and will be more discerning, so you will benefit more.

Moreover, when you do finally read them, our suggestion is that you read at least one in depth and perhaps skim as many as half a dozen others from different (and even threatening) theological perspectives. This will help you to pick up things you might have missed, deepening your understanding of the text. By all means read and listen to the commentators; they will be of significant help in various places. However, don't be afraid to disagree on the basis of your own reading of the Scriptures.

## Growing in Submission to Scripture

One thing to notice about the Pastoral Epistles is that they do not urge the leaders of God's people only to *know* the Scriptures well and to teach them well to others. They also urge them to *apply* those Scriptures to themselves. Moreover, when leaders of God's people are being chosen, they are to be people who do this. If we return to 1 Timothy, this is obvious in the advice Paul gives Timothy about choosing overseers and deacons in chapter 3. The striking thing about the list of traits that congregations should look for is the relative absence of gifts and the prevalence of godly attributes that are demonstrated in life. Such traits include having a good married and family life, being self-controlled, and not being given to excesses or inappropriate use of things such as alcohol, money, and argument or use of the tongue. Leaders are not simply to be devoted to teaching the truth of the Scriptures to God's people and to outsiders. They are also to be good husbands, godly fathers, nonmanipulative leaders, models of godly living, and those who have a good reputation with outsiders. Obviously this would be true not only of those engaged in oversight of congregations, but of all who minister the word of God to the people of God in the variety of contexts in which this happens in the contemporary church.

Nearly every pastor we know can give examples of once godly friends who went through theological training with them or worked in churches nearby, but who are no longer in ministry (or, in some cases, not even in the faith) because of sins of a moral or relational kind. Guarding our lives and our teaching is therefore a constant need, one that is captured in the apostle's advice to Timothy:

> Practice these things, immerse yourself in them, so that all may see your progress. Keep a close watch on yourself and on the teaching. Persist in this, for by so doing you will save both yourself and your hearers. (1 Tim. 4:15–16)

The four imperatives are important: (1) practice these things, (2) immerse yourself in them, (3) keep a close watch, and (4) persist. Basically, Paul is exhorting Timothy to focus on the teachings and duties that Paul has laid out in the previous verses, to take care of his conduct and his teaching.

Such exhortations make clear that guarding our lives and our teaching is a constant need that requires vigilance and focus. This can be helped by meeting with others to urge one another on and to keep one another accountable. It might even mean setting rigid boundaries for ourselves that help us avoid drifting in these areas. God's leaders are to be people who are growing in submission to Scripture. Their daily lives are to reflect and exemplify the Scriptures that they teach. We are to be those with whom there is no hint or appearance of evil (1 Thess. 5:21–22).

What might this mean in practice? If you are heading a team, it might mean issuing constant reminders of such things and fearlessly keeping your team members accountable (or requiring them to be accountable to others) in these areas. Moreover, you should eschew any fear of setting helpful unbreakable rules for yourself and of telling others about them. Apart from anything else, this will be an example to others to set similar boundaries. In the area of doctrine, you might have set habits for reading the Bible, reading theology, and meeting with others who can hold you accountable theologically. In terms of godliness, you might set some appropriate and public boundaries in terms of meeting with others of the opposite sex (such as never meeting privately in a closed environment, such as a windowless office). You might agree with your spouse that either one of you will tell the other if you ever feel attracted to someone else. Whatever you do, recognize that you are what the Bible says, a sinful human, and therefore needy of not just divine help but also wise advice. Using the advice of Psalm 1, don't even start walking in the counsel of the wicked lest in the end you find yourself standing in the way of sinners and finally sitting in the seat of scoffers (and sharing their fate).

As preachers of God's word, we should be aiming not only to be effective and godly communicators of the word, but also godly practitioners, particularly in the task of being pastor-teachers of God's people.

## Becoming a Person of Consistent and Devoted Prayerfulness

While the narratives contained in Matthew and Mark record the Lord praying regularly, Luke takes a particular interest in Jesus's occasions for prayer, as well as the practices of the early church in prayer. For example, Jesus prays at his baptism (Luke 3:21) and withdraws to pray at significant moments, sometimes—but not always—with his disciples (e.g., 6:12; 9:18, 28–29; 11:1). He urges his disciples to pray for laborers for the harvest (10:2) and for the kingdom (11:1–4), and to not lose heart in prayer (18:1). He tells a parable that urges the disciples and the people to pray properly (18:9–14), and he warns them of the need for prayer in view of the coming kingdom, that they might stand appropriately before the Son of Man on that day (21:34–36). On top of all of this, in his approach to his betrayal, trial, and death, he prays for his disciples to stay faithful, encourage one another, and have strength to stay awake and stand firm (21:34–36; 22:46); for Simon Peter to come through his sifting by Satan (22:31–32); and for himself in his submission to the will of God (22:41–44). Such a proliferation of records of our Lord praying indicates his utter dependence on bringing to his Father all matters of his life and ministry, as well as that of his disciples.

Luke then recalls how the disciples and those who benefitted from their ministry followed Jesus's example. They prayed about the replacement of Judas (Acts 1:24–25), for the seven who were appointed to serve at tables (6:1–6), for the Samaritans who received the word of God (8:14–17), and about numerous other events throughout the book of Acts, such that the whole book is punctuated by prayer. Through such reporting, Luke demonstrates the critical importance and frequency of prayer in the ministry of the early church. His record clearly indicates that such is normal for a people engaged with God in the ministry of bringing others to the knowledge of Jesus, then helping them grow in love for him and in bearing his gospel to the world.

The pastor who is seeking to bring the word of God to the people of God and to people who do not yet know him therefore must be a person of prayer. Charles Spurgeon is even stronger than this. He says that among "all the formative influences which go to make up a man honored of God in the ministry," he knows "of none more mighty than his familiarity with the mercy seat" of God. He goes on to say:

> All that a college course can do for a student is coarse and external compared with the spiritual and delicate refinement obtained by communion with God. While the unformed minister is revolving upon the wheel of preparation, prayer is the tool of the great potter by which he moulds the vessel. All our libraries and studies are mere emptiness compared to our closets. We grow, we wax mightily, we prevail in private prayer.
>
> Your prayers will be your ablest assistants *while your discourses are yet upon the anvil.* . . . The commentators are good instructors, but the Author Himself is far better, and prayer makes a direct appeal to him and enlists Him in our cause. It is a great thing to pray one's self into the spirit and marrow of a text; working into it by sacred feeding thereon, even as the worm bores its way into the kernel of the nut.[1]

While the language is strong, vibrant, and perhaps more poetic than some of us can handle, the thrust has great truth for the preacher. Our studies and preparation are to be places of consistent and devoted prayer, depending on God our Father, through his Spirit, to make his word known to his people as we,

---

1. Charles H. Spurgeon, *Lectures to My Students: A Selection from Addresses Delivered to the Students of the Pastors' College, Metropolitan Tabernacle, Vol. 1, Lecture III* (London: Passmore and Alabaster, 1875), 41–42. Emphasis original.

in weakness, proclaim the strength of his Son in the power of the same Spirit.

## Growing as a Communicator of Different Types of Texts

All preachers, like most readers of Scripture, have favorite parts of the Bible. While one of us is most at home with narrative, either Old or New Testament, our impression is that most of our friends or those who come from theological backgrounds similar to ours are most at home with the Pauline Epistles. The difficulty is that not all texts preach like the Pauline Epistles, and therefore we need to learn different ways of communicating that are sympathetic to the genres of the passages we are preaching from. This might mean learning how to engage affectively as well as cognitively and learning how to be a storyteller as well as an explainer. Learning to immerse our people into the poetry of Scripture might mean learning to engage emotions and not just the mind. God has presumably caused Scripture to be written in a variety of genres because he knows that different genres work for different people and/or in different situations, and that certain types of writing are better for communicating certain truths than others (we touched on this at the end of chap. 7). We now need to recognize how this reality might be reflected in our preaching as we learn to grow as able communicators of different types of texts. How can we develop as preachers of narrative texts, apocalyptic literature, parables, Wisdom Literature, the Epistles, and prophecy, recognizing that our standard template might not be right for each? It would take another book to explore this question, so all we can do here is flag its importance for the long-haul or lifelong preacher.

Perhaps we can capture something of the need in the following way. A good sermon is not only a sermon that tells people what a passage meant for its original audience, how it fits into God's purposes in Christ, what it means for its contemporary audience, and how God wants it to change them. It should *also* work hard to persuade an audience to change not just their thinking and actions appropriately, but also their affections and feelings in a way that is sympathetic to the genre of the passage. To give an example, were we preaching on David's sin in 2 Samuel 11–12, we might want our hearers to see the awfulness of David's sin, but also perhaps to feel the depth of his repentance and its meaning by tapping into his reflection on his emotions as expressed in Psalm 51. This might drive people to engage with the depth of their own sin and their need for rigorous and deep repentance.

## Long-Term Preaching Ministries

As we have considered the ministries of preachers who have had significant personal, local, and even international impact (e.g., those of John Calvin, Charles Simeon, Charles Spurgeon, John Stott, John Piper, and Philip Jensen), there is an element that appears common in many of them: they were based largely in one place for a long time. Even if it is not possible for you, for one reason or another, to be in one place for as long as some of these men, it is still not out of the question, and it is also possible these days for many preachers entering the ministry of the word to have time to preach through the whole Bible. Yet, the pastoral benefits of a long-term ministry placement are as great as the educational benefits, because it allows extensive time to follow through with people. Long-term ministries open up doorways into people's lives that might otherwise only be cracks of light.

Imagine that it is possible for you to be in one place for a long time and that you have finally decided you have enough experience and knowledge to take on a series on the book of Zechariah. You begin to preach and finally arrive at chapter 14, where the language can be very disturbing for some people. The chapter opens with a prophecy of the nations gathered by God to judge his people. The results are terrifying: the city is captured, houses are ransacked, and women are raped. Such graphic imagery and language might particularly mean that people need time to talk to their pastor about this. Moreover, there might be some who have been sexually assaulted or abused, and for whom the language will be very confronting. If you have been the pastor for a long time, you or your colleagues may very well know the people who might be deeply affected and be able to either warn them about the sermon beforehand or be ready to specifically talk to them after you preach this passage.

In a similar vein, what about when you are preaching through Samuel? In the very first chapter we are introduced to Hannah, of whom we are told (twice) that God has given her no children. Then God does grant her a child in response to her prayers. However, in our congregations we are sure to have women (and men) struggling with infertility who have prayed endlessly that God might grant them children, but they remain childless. They too might need to speak with someone after hearing Hannah's story. If you have female staff members who know the situation, you might even key them in beforehand about the issues of the passage and ask them to keep an eye out and be available to those who might find the passage disturbing.

In both situations outlined above, particularly if your ministry has been a long-term one, you or other staff members might have journeyed with the people of the church over many years. You might already be aware of some of the potential feelings that they might have to the preaching of a given passage, and might be able to follow up intentionally. You might even decide that the sermon could be too overwhelming for them in their current situation, so you might warn them ahead of time that it could be difficult. Perhaps you could give them permission to not be there if you think that things might be too tender for them, given the place they are in at the moment (and possibly undertake to explain your reasons and the passage to them personally at a later date). A long-term tenure at a single church allows such insight and trust, and so adds benefit to pastoral care.

Another advantage of a long-term ministry is the space to bring up things that cannot possibly be dealt with in one sermon but to which you might return later, perhaps even designing a further sermon or series of sermons to deal with such things in greater depth. For the congregation, the theological consistency afforded by having the same pastor preach to them over an extended period of time is immeasurable. Even if subsequent pastors have the same broad theological position, each will have his own idiosyncrasies and stylistic differences that the church will need to get used to, and none will have the same long train of thought that has been sharing minds and lives with the people over many years.

However, despite the advantages, staying in one place and exercising a long-term ministry there is not easy. It requires stamina. It also demands good principles and practices of refreshment. You need to work out how to be refreshed, how to persevere.

In all of this, it is critically important to recognize that we are different from the world. Strong biblical pastoral ministry is not about career advancement, as in many secular jobs. It is about self-sacrificial caring for God's people and nurturing them as God's representative shepherd. Congregations and our preaching are not stepping-stones to other things or a means to other ends, such as our careers. This is made clear in places such as Ezekiel 34, which talks about the rotten shepherds of God's people who were not there for the advantage of the sheep. Rather, the sheep were a means to an end. Your people must know that you seek to be a shepherd like God and his Son. You want to search for the lost, bring back the strays, bind up the injured, and strengthen the weak even as God himself does (Ezek. 34:12–16).

For some, long-term ministries are simply not possible, either because of their makeup, God's particular gifting, or even family reasons. However, that does not mean that the things explained above do not apply. Even if we do not stay in one place for the long term, that does not mean that we cannot think long term or have a long-term orientation. Our locations might change, but we can have a long-term focus. For example, we can think and preach with our eyes on the long-term growth of our present and future congregations rather than spending thirty or more years recycling the same sermons over and over again and not growing in our understanding of God and of ourselves in the light of his word.

God has gifted one of us to start new things or fix things that are broken. When preaching, he acts as though he is in it for the long term. Moreover, while he occasionally might reuse old sermons, the goal has always been to be working on new parts of the Bible. Sometimes this practice is guided by the particular matters needed for a new context. At other times, it is guided by his own need to continue to grow in his understanding of Scripture and its application to the people to whom he is ministering. It is not always easy to disentangle these multiple interests, but they are not mutually exclusive. His priority has therefore always been preaching new books of the Bible that are particularly applicable to the people to whom he is ministering.

## Other Matters for Long-Term Ministries

A long-term ministry not only provides benefits for preaching, but also provides benefits in terms of thinking and planning. It can allow you to seriously think about how to produce and follow through with a next generation of pastor-teachers, either for the church you're at, the church plants that might flow from it, the revitalization of the denomination of which you are a part, or Christ's church in all the world. You can draw in others of like mind, produce others of like mind, and perhaps even bring significant reformation. Of course, there's a negative spin-off as well, and that is the risk that the ministry's faults will also be replicated or even made worse.

A long-term ministry also often grows strong financially, perhaps because people get to know their pastor better and align themselves with his vision for a church. Additionally, he knows them better and is therefore better equipped to speak into their lives both at a personal and corporate level. Such financial strength can be used for God's kingdom, helping less fortunate churches with developing training or providing mentoring and training of future preachers. Stability can also mean strengthening and maintaining consistency in missions. Constructive thought and money can be given to training preachers for parts of the world where preaching is poor and preachers have no opportunity for mentoring and training. Such are just a few of the possibilities that are open for strong long-term ministries as compared to shorter and less stable ministries.

## A Final Point for the Disorganized or Organizationally Challenged

Throughout this book, we have been speaking about a very detailed, long-term, integrated paradigm of preaching and church leadership. This chapter has deliberately been a bit more discursive and has more widely reflected on the personal implications, responsibilities, and opportunities that come about as you begin to think and plan long term as we have urged. Of course, that raises another question: "What if I am an organizationally challenged, more spontaneous sort of person?"

The quick response, but probably the best one, is to urge you to start to get organized. Start disciplining yourself in terms of organization. No matter what else happens, this is important. However, if you know you can preach and can make that happen each week, but you could not organize your way out of a paper bag, then find someone who can help. The best solution we have found is to identify an able administrator who is theologically trained in a manner that lines up with your own theological convictions and who is committed to local church ministry. You might have a person with the gifts but not the theological education. If so, send him off to theological college for that training and then bring him back to work with you. Alternatively, ask like-minded friends whether they know of someone suitable. Interview very carefully and over a good period of time. Make sure that there is agreement and an ability to work together. Take this person on board and equip him to help you and help organize you and others. Keep him as a colleague and confidant as well. Build up a long-term friendship and partnership. Listen and be willing to be rebuked and helped when necessary.

## 12

# Congregational Care

Throughout this book, we have spoken about an approach to preaching that may be radically different from what many pastors are used to, and we have explored many of the logistics and implications of deciding to preach this way. Necessarily, this has meant that the focus has been on the preacher and his works of ministry. But Christian ministry is not ultimately about program management, it is about people. Programs are good only insofar as they help real people. In this final chapter, we will offer a few reflections on how we can bring our congregations with us as we make the shift to preaching through the whole Bible.

## Teaching about How You Are Teaching

It is one thing for the preacher to decide that he is going to establish a preaching program that works through the entire Bible over several decades. It is another thing for his congregation to embrace that plan. Because few churches have a history of this kind of preaching, the idea of, say, a ten-week preaching series through Leviticus might be something that some members of the congregation balk at—and that reaction might be intensified when they learn that this is just the first of several consecutive preaching series on Leviticus! It is therefore important for a preacher to help members of the church understand why he has chosen to do things this way. Put simply, the members of the congregation need to understand the value of studying the whole counsel of God over the course of their lives or they will not be interested in doing it. There are three things to bear in mind when trying to grow a church in this conviction.

First, it may be important to outline some of the basic Christian beliefs regarding the nature of the Bible. There are a cluster of related doctrines about Scripture that together make sense of the priority that Christians ascribe to it, including the doctrines of inspiration, perspicuity, inerrancy, sufficiency, and authority. All of these sound technical, which might put some people off, but their basic substance is not too difficult for anyone to grasp. (*Inspiration* means that the Bible is God's word, and it was written as the Holy Spirit worked in, with, and through human authors. *Perspicuity* means that the Bible is clear in what it says. *Inerrancy* means that the Bible is without fault. *Sufficiency* means that while the Bible may not tell us everything we want to know about everything, it is sufficient for salvation and to guide holy and faithful living that is centered on Jesus. *Authority* means that the Bible is to be received as the word of God to us.) Any preacher who has had formal theological training at a reputable mainstream seminary should be able to explain these beliefs to his congregation. Of course, this does not mean that he must do this by preaching doctrinal sermons about the nature of the Bible. Although we do agree that there can be some occasions for topical sermons, it might be that other forums are more appropriate for establishing some of these baseline assumptions. Perhaps the church could produce a leaflet outlining its convictions about the Bible and therefore about preaching. Also, this information might be posted on the church's website. Or the pastors might clearly outline the church's convictions and derivative practice at its regular welcome evenings for newcomers. There are a number of ways to communicate the driving beliefs about the Scriptures.

Second, it is important to move a congregation from having the right technical information about the Bible to *loving* the Bible. Few people get passionate about raw facts that are only held in their heads, not having a place in their hearts. And, interestingly, there is much in the Bible itself that highlights not just its inspiration, inerrancy, authority, and so on, but also its beauty, and the great joy of knowing God's words and living by them. A classic example of this is Psalm 19:7–11, which says,

> The law of the LORD is perfect,
>     reviving the soul;
> the testimony of the LORD is sure,
>     making wise the simple;
> the precepts of the LORD are right,
>     rejoicing the heart;
> the commandment of the LORD is pure,
>     enlightening the eyes;
> the fear of the LORD is clean,
>     enduring forever;
> the rules of the LORD are true,
>     and righteous altogether.
> More to be desired are they than gold,
>     even much fine gold;
> sweeter also than honey
>     and drippings of the honeycomb.
> Moreover, by them is your servant warned;
>     in keeping them there is great reward.

These are not the precise and logically connected words of the systematic theologian, but rather the passionate outpourings of the poet, and they reflect not just a set of correct beliefs about the Bible, but a deep and heartfelt affection for it.[1]

---

1. See Peter Adam, *Written for Us: Receiving God's Words in the Bible* (Nottingham, UK: Inter-Varsity, 2008), 109–15.

It is generally important for church members to have a healthy balance of head and heart, one reason being that it affects their openness to hearing the whole Bible preached. A congregation that is "all head" may be more interested in hearing a series of talks on the rational proofs for God than the Leviticus series. One that is "all heart" may just want to get lost in singing long sets of anthemic songs. But the Bible shows us that God's people should have a passion for his word; the affections of the heart should be directed toward the goodness of the Bible. It is good for a church to foster this kind of love for the Bible through the ways in which the members speak about it to one another and by having the Bible prioritized in their corporate activities. The more the Bible is championed, the more it is valued.

Being honest, it is a little sad to find preachers who have a correct but dry appreciation of the Scriptures. Admirably, these sorts of preachers often strive to protect the objective facts about, and within, the Bible, many of which have been under heavy assault in recent decades. But this defense of the truth need not come at the expense of a subjective appreciation of the word of God; both should go together. The reality is that congregations respond to a preacher's passions as much as to his logic, and so being shameless and expressive about our love for the Bible is likely to be more infectious than simply being right.

Third, preachers can actually foster their people's love for the Bible simply by preaching through it in the way we are arguing for in this book. It might be that there really is not a great deal of surface enthusiasm for the Leviticus series at first. But, God willing, as the congregation learns more about the different offerings required under the old covenant and the different ways in which Jesus fulfills them all, the people should start to grow in their interest in Leviticus. As they consider the problems of unintentional individual and corporate sin, and the sufficiency of Christ's death for these, they should begin to develop an excitement about the ways Leviticus engages so much of the human predicament that is part of their own experience. And then, as they see that the old covenant priests were given specific instructions as to how they could mediate for the people, and that this work foreshadowed the final mediations of Jesus, they should come to love the way in which the opening chapters of Leviticus lie behind, fit right into, and thicken up their understanding of the ways the whole Bible tells the great story of Jesus in incredibly rich ways. Experiencing Leviticus preached should grow love not only of Leviticus, but of the Bible as a whole. Of course, the great merit in this approach of letting the text create love for the text is that it can always be happening, week by week. This means that regular, long-term members of the church, first-time visitors, and everyone in between will be learning, and having reinforced, the goodness and beauty of the Bible.

## Mixed Congregations in Constant Flux

Many churches have a slightly different attendance each week, with visitors passing through, regular members absent for various reasons, long-term members moving away for good, contract workers coming and going, and "fringe" people dropping by with differing degrees of predictability. This variable attendance can create great challenges for preachers who are working hard to feed their flock a balanced diet of Scripture. Indeed, some preachers might find this fluctuation reason enough to abandon the idea of long-term planning altogether, reasoning instead that if they just make sure that every sermon they preach is true to the passage it is taken from, that will have to do.

Of course, it is true that patchy attendance decreases the value of carefully developed seriatim sermon series, and few people have perfect attendance records, but we would make the point again that we believe it is far better to aim high and fall short than to aim low and succeed. A family who eats a balanced diet for even just half of their meals will be better off than a family who abandons any attempt at all to plan a thoughtful menu. It would be hard to argue that the visitor who hears only a single gospel-focused expository sermon from, say, the middle of a series on Hebrews is going to be worse off than if he or she had heard a one-off sermon from somewhere else. And the rest of the congregation will benefit so much more from the ongoing expository approach to preaching.

Not only does attendance change week by week, but the regular and committed members of the congregation are at different places in their spiritual lives. Some might be regular seekers who are not yet converted to Christ, but are very interested in learning more. Others might be young in the faith, perhaps because of their age or because they have only recently made commitments to Jesus. Some might be seasoned believers with ten or twenty years of discipleship behind them. And some might be elderly, having trusted in and served the Lord for decades and decades, and now faithfully waiting for their time to go to him. Those in the last group might also have been in the church far, far longer than the preacher. Of course, things are still more complicated, as each year seekers become believers, the young get older, the elderly die, and so on.

In addition to all of this, we are never dealing with homogenous groups, but each individual who comes to church on Sunday has his or her own particular background and story, and has different things going on in his or her life. Along with everything already noted, there might also be seminary students, people struggling with singleness, married couples with young families, widows, ex-prisoners, victims of abuse, people who are very sick, people from a range of ethnic backgrounds, people who are not very fluent in the language you are preaching in, people who are loving life, people who are lazy, people carrying a burden of guilt, people not repenting of some sins, people with different theological convictions, academics, unemployed people, working-class folk, and visitors about whom you know nothing. The possibilities are endless.

The first problem that this presents to a preacher is not tied to the goal of preaching through the whole Bible in seriatim series, but is actually related to preaching any sermon at all. Is it possible to preach in such a way that a highly diverse group of people is taught, exhorted, encouraged, and grown? Some preachers might suggest that while this is indeed difficult, there are certain sorts of sermons with which it is more conceivable: those with a near-universal message. That message, of course, is the gospel, and so the way to address the "problem" of a mixed congregation is just to preach simple gospel messages. (We are actually very reluctant to call a mixed congregation a problem, as we believe it is a fantastic expression of the power of the gospel to bring diverse people together.) But that "solution" might create one of a number of new problems, including the preacher running out of simple gospel texts, artificially shoehorning a certain doctrinal paradigm onto texts where it is not naturally found, and failing to preach the Scriptures with much breadth or depth. If the preacher's goal is to preach the gospel only in a narrowly conceived way, he runs the risk of making this a priority at the expense of the fullness of the biblical texts before him.

Some churches include special evangelistic sermons as part of their preaching programs, as we noted earlier. For these, they often break from the pattern of expository preaching to offer sermons pitched especially to unbelievers, whom the pastors hope the congregation will make a special effort to invite on the weeks when these sermons are preached. This is a very well-motivated practice, and it is hard to find fault with a desire to evangelize. However, there is a particular drawback to this pattern—it can lead members to think that only certain biblical texts or certain types of sermons clearly communicate the message of Christ. It also suggests that regular weekly preaching in the church is somewhat decoupled from the gospel message, and that some parts of the Bible are for outsiders and others are for insiders. As is evident in our sample preaching program in chapter 8, we do not believe that it is necessary to split the preaching program to include such specifically evangelistic sermons, but would prefer that the gospel be communicated through every sermon. To be sure, this can allow the preacher to address certain points to specific groups in his sermons, but he can do this without unhelpfully targeting sermons to some groups and thereby excluding others.

A far better approach is to continue preaching through the whole Bible theologically, as we discussed in chapter 5. This allows the gospel to be highlighted from every part of the Bible without the sermons becoming predictably repetitious. It also has the benefit of offering milk to those who are young in the faith or have not yet grasped the gospel, and meat to more established believers who might be surprised to find new facets, layers, and connections to the central message of Jesus in all parts of the Bible. We must remember that maturing in the faith does not mean moving on from the message that converts to some other, more sophisticated teaching, but rather comprehending ever more of the breadth, length, height, and depth of the love of Christ, who is our Lord and risen-from-death Savior. This thickening up of our congregations' knowledge and understanding of the works of God centered on Jesus is also what helps them face all of the various trials of life, be they singleness, sickness, or the seductions of sin. Perhaps counterintuitively, this approach may also be more evangelistically effective, as preaching from across the breadth of the Bible might connect with more of the felt needs of unbelievers and therefore serve to provide different access points to the gospel or to remove different "defeater" beliefs that have obscured the gospel. It will always be important for seekers to hear an unambiguous and directed call to faith, but it may not be that this must be the first or only thing they hear from the pulpit. God can connect different parts of his word to different parts of their lives as part of his work of drawing them progressively closer to himself.

Along with being thoughtful about what is most effective in evangelistic sermons, preachers must also recognize the importance of preaching those parts of the Scriptures that do not seem to intersect with many of the regular congregation's immediate felt needs. Although it may not be apparent at the time, we know that those passages were written for the good of God's people, so they are ignored at some cost. While a young, healthy couple might wonder about the relevance to them of John 5:1–9, where Jesus heals a man who has been an invalid for thirty-eight years, they need to hear its message so that they are ready to faithfully deal with chronic sickness if they do face it in later life, and so that they are able to more empathetically understand and share the good news with others who are in circumstances different from their own. Going further still, it is not just for pragmatic equipping or preparation that preachers should proclaim the "less immediately relevant" texts, but also because one outcome of preaching through the whole Bible is that the congregation's entire worldview is shaped. That is, the object of sitting under the whole counsel of God is not just to learn a million separate facts and points of application, but to have our minds transformed to think in God's ways about all of life.

One seasoned preacher (and gifted musician) we know compared this process to learning to play the piano. He said that after taking ten years of piano classes, no one actually remembers many of the individual lessons. The piano student cannot say that she learned a certain chord voicing on a certain day or a certain scale on another. But she can certainly play. She has been shaped as a person who can sit down at a keyboard, put her fingers on the keys, and make beautiful music. Similarly, the Christian who sits for years under sermons that are part of a well-thought-through preaching program will be able to live beautifully to God's glory in much of what life brings to her. This is not necessarily because she always remembers certain applications from certain sermons, but because she has been soaked in great swaths of biblical texts that have given her a profoundly Christian mind-set and outlook on life in all its diversity.

It may sound challenging to preach well to a mixed and ever-changing group, but it is not impossible, and it is probably a necessary skill for most preachers to develop. It may actually be possible to glean some tips about how to do this from other media. For example, many of the newer animated children's movies have much for parents and adults expertly woven in. While the surface story and presentation quickly engage young viewers, many adults deeply appreciate the artistic quality of the productions, and there are often underlying themes that only more mature minds appreciate, as well as any number of jokes and pop-culture references that go straight over kids' heads. The makers of these films know that while their primary audience is children, many of those children are able to go to the cinema only with an accompanying adult. They are therefore wise to make a film that everyone can enjoy, even if in different ways. There are also lots of storybooks, toys (Lego probably being one of the best examples), and events that do similar things. Preachers have different goals and motivations, but can learn much from these types of examples of connecting with a mixed audience.

## Preaching to *Your* Congregation

Finally, and very importantly, we must comment about the importance of preachers preaching to their own congregations. By this we mean that they should avoid falling into the trap of preaching to either an absent or imaginary audience.

Many churches these days record each week's sermon and make it available via their websites or podcasts. This is hugely beneficial for those members of a church who, for one reason or another, are not able to be at church each week, and especially if the church is committed to preaching seriatim series. In the past, it has been far more difficult for absent members to catch up on sermons and thereby keep pace with a series that was sequentially teaching through every chapter and verse of a given book of the Bible. Nowadays, to do so is relatively simple, and is so helpful that it would seem a shame for a church not to have an audio ministry for this purpose. Furthermore, in addition to serving temporarily absent members, online sermons can be a great gift to people who live or work in remote areas where it is never easy to get to a church with regularity. For those in such situations, access to good online sermons can be a real lifeline. It is also great for preachers to have access to recorded sermons by other and greater preachers, as listening to, and reflecting upon, these can help with continual growth and development in the art and science of preaching.

But there is a shadow side to the posting of sermons online—the temptation for the preacher to preach for the unknown potential masses "out there" who might subscribe to the podcast or head to the website to listen live or download past sermons. In doing this, he is not prioritizing the particular needs of his own congregation at that particular moment. Instead of having the church roll in front of him as he prepares his sermons, he has one eye on the statistics page of the church website. When this is the focus, he is not reflecting on the ways that the text of the week speaks into the current happenings and circumstances of his people, but instead is operating at a more generic level, seeking to apply the text broadly rather than specifically. This both impoverishes the congregation and offers the virtual congregation only something untailored. It fails to speak to the situations that the preacher should know about, and tries to speak to people in situations the preacher cannot know about. It is a far cry from knowing the flock by name and using this knowledge to serve them. Preaching for the absent audience can also lead to the temptation to not preach the entire Bible on the calculation that even if, say, Amos 6 is the next passage in an ongoing series, a sermon on that chapter is less likely to attract wide outside interest than a sermon on Romans 3 or one entitled "Jesus the Miracle Worker."

It takes only a moment to realize that underlying much of this discussion is the ugly reality of pride. It is sadly true that many Christian preachers thrive on the praise of other people rather than the grace of God, and that preachers too often foster hopes of becoming recognized among the ranks of the great ones. This is terribly worldly, even though what is being evaluated is ostensibly spiritual. Seeking the accolades attached to being the most downloaded preacher on the internet or the go-to speaker at that large Christian event in your city is no better than seeking the accolades attached to being the most downloaded political theorist on the internet or the go-to speaker at that large secular event in your city. When the motivation is self-promotion rather than honoring God and serving people, the discipline is irrelevant.

Closely related to pride is jealousy, and this can be born out of a dissatisfaction with the place where God has called us. Instead of faithfully and thankfully laboring away at preaching through the Bible for a smallish congregation in a smallish town, we can instead look to the capital cities, with their megachurches and high-profile pastors, and think about how we could preach ourselves into contention for a role alongside them. In doing this, we are forgetting that God has us exactly where he wants us and that he is as pleased with us doing our work of feeding our particular flock the fullness of his word as he is with the megachurch pastor proclaiming the gospel to thousands each week. In fact, if we were not preaching the word of God to the members of our flock, they might miss out on it, and so what we are doing is essential in God's economy. God has marked out some to be famous stadium preachers, so we can peacefully entrust that task to them. He has entrusted others of us with the various flocks and missions we have, so that is where we must concentrate our efforts.

It is not only the unknown masses whose praises we can covet. We recently heard a very sad story of a church's new associate pastor coming to realize after about two years in his role that he had been preparing his sermons in ways that he thought would impress his former seminary lecturers. Of course, none of his seminary lecturers actually attended his church, so it is unlikely that he caught their attention, but the real problem was again that he was not preaching with the people of his congregation in his mind or on his heart. To his great credit, he was perceptive and humble enough to self-diagnose his error and has since made the necessary changes in the mind-set he brings to his preparation, but his story is a warning to all preachers. Our goal in preaching is to serve, not to impress. In the weekly cut and thrust of church life, there are no marks on offer for excellent sermon craft. This is not to say that we should not be striving to prepare excellent sermons; of course we should. But it is to say that as we prayerfully work hard to bring the whole message of God to the people of God, we must not focus on the attention we get for doing it, but on the particular people for whom God has made us preachers. They are the ones who need our ministry, and as much as our seminary lecturers or other heroes in the faith might benefit from our expositions, they have their own churches where they are fed with the Scriptures by their own pastors.

It is also unhealthy for people to learn from the Bible only online, by broadcast, or by recordings. Not only is the teaching generically rather than specifically applied, but the local church can be undermined too. There are too many cases of congregation members disengaging from the preaching of their own churches because they have found preferred alternatives online. In the worst cases, these people cannot endure sound teaching, but having itching ears, they accumulate for themselves teachers to suit their own passions, turn away from the truth, and wander off into myths (2 Tim. 4:3–4). Where this is the case, the pastoral team needs to lovingly warn and call back the offender. But in many cases, there is no theological problem with the online preacher; the real issue is just the inappropriate disempowering of the local preacher and devaluing of local church cohesion. Although it might be true that most of us who preach through the Bible week by week lack the mastery of the great and famous preachers, we do have a particular concern for, and personal knowledge of, our people that cannot be matched by a celebrity pastor. We can therefore speak into their lives in ways that the online voice cannot. We also have a heart for the common life of the church, and there is a particular experience of unity that comes from a local gathering of believers all studying the same part of Scripture at the same time. This unity can also be more than a vague positive feeling; we have seen how it can also be dovetailed with the church's current ministry plans. Therefore, when members check out and opt for alternative sources of preaching, they not only disperse the common mind, they can also de-energize local gospel works.

The downside of listening to too many online sermons can be illustrated by a thought experiment that takes the situation to its extreme. What would happen if we identified the very best preacher in the world, recorded him preaching through the entire Bible, translated those recordings into all the languages of the world, and then used only these resources to teach all the believers in all of the churches of the world, abandoning all other preaching? Would we be better or worse off? Clearly, there would be immeasurably huge savings of time and money, as we would not need to employ any more preachers ever again. But we would have made preaching so generic and impersonal that one of the results would be a mass detachment of the people of the church from the life of the ministry of the word of God. People need a preacher who is present with them, and who knows and cares for them, to bring the whole word of God to bear on their lives. We all need someone who knows when our community needs to hear the book of James and when we need to study Numbers. We need someone who realizes that Jeremiah 46 will touch a nerve and why, and who is ready to follow up the preaching of this text with pastoral visits to work through its implications. Our churches need preachers who can speak to us as collected groups of unique individuals who yet share some particular commonalities of time, place, and circumstance that bond and shape us in ways that are different from any other gathering of God's people. We need preachers who are pastors of those people, and we need the pastors of those people to be preachers.

# Conclusion

Numbers 20:2–13 records an incident in the period after the Israelites had been freed from slavery in Egypt and were wandering in the wilderness as they slowly moved toward the promised land. As they had done before, the people argued with Moses and Aaron, and complained about being brought into a barren and harsh environment that did not have enough water to sustain the nation and its animals. Moses and Aaron brought this concern before the Lord in prayer, and the Lord responded by telling them to assemble the people before a rock and then to tell that rock to yield water for them. Moses and Aaron followed these directions, although instead of simply speaking to the rock, Moses chose to strike it twice with his staff. While God still showed his power and grace at this moment by letting water flow abundantly from the rock for the people, he also rebuked Moses for the manner in which he had acted. God had directed Moses to speak to the rock, but Moses hit it instead. Although it might seem like a small thing to us, Moses was disobedient in striking the rock—and his actions perhaps indicated that he was questioning God's capacity to work through calm words alone—so he was judged by God.

It is the particular nature of his punishment and his subsequent actions that are interesting to us at this point. The punishment God declared was that Moses would not be the one to lead the people into the promised land; he had forfeited that honor and blessing. We later find that what God spoke was exactly what came to pass. Moses died on the verge of the land, and Joshua was established as leader of the nation in his place and took the Israelites across the Jordan River and into Canaan. It is easy to imagine Moses feeling devastated at his punishment. After all he had done in confronting the power of Pharaoh face to face, meeting with God on Mount Sinai, taking responsibility for a recurrently sinful and ungrateful people, and living in the dry desert for years and years, he was not going to be allowed to enter the land flowing with milk and honey at the end of the journey. He was to miss out on the prize for which he had worked so long and hard. It is therefore also possible to imagine Moses simply giving up at this point and quitting his position. Once God had said that he would not reach the goal, he could have become so disheartened, discouraged, and disinterested in his task that he abandoned it altogether, concluding that if he could not lead the people all of the way, there was no point in leading them anywhere further at all. Of course, as we read forward to the end of Deuteronomy, we find that he did not do this at all, but instead accepted God's judgment and continued in the task that had been set for him, taking the people as far as he could before entrusting their care to someone else.

This story serves as a great parallel to our need to strive toward feeding the people of God who are entrusted to us with the whole counsel of God, even if we do not believe we will be able to complete the entire task in the course of our ministries. We might be tempted to feel that if we cannot go all the way, there is no point in even making a start because an incomplete project is a worthless project. But the truth is that it is actually better to labor on and bring people ever closer to the promised land than to abandon them in the wilderness. It is better to set the course toward our destination and chart it truly for as far as we can go than to not set out at all. It is better to feed our congregations with as much of the word of God as we are able, even if it does not end up that we preach every single chapter and verse ourselves. There is real value in starting this project, even if we leave it unfinished or pass it on at the end of our preaching careers.

In fact, even if we are now already approaching the end of our years in preaching, it will still be better for us to preach through one whole book of the Bible that our people have not sat under before than to just repreach a section of the Gospels that we have already looked at with them several times. There is no doubt that members of the church would benefit from hearing Matthew 5–7 again, but the argument of this book is that they are likely to benefit even more from hearing, say, Hosea preached through for the first time. The Matthew texts may reiterate things that are good not to forget, but the Hosea sermons might open up some very new and surprisingly relevant thoughts from the mind of God. In addition to feeding the flock more fully, even a relatively short preaching ministry that is designed around a plan to preach the whole Bible can also be very significant in setting the church's culture and expectations. After hearing the Hosea sermon series and thereby having their appetites whetted for more of God's word, the members of the church are more likely to understand, and even welcome, the decision of our successor when he steps up to preach through Micah. Like Joshua following Moses, the new pastor will be able to pick up and continue on a good work well established, because he will not need to begin setting the paradigm or start working through all of the Bible's books from scratch. Our work will not have been pointless or wasted; rather, it will have been a substantial contribution to the healthy spiritual lives of our congregations.

From the very start of this book we have acknowledged that many preachers may not be able to complete the whole task of preaching through the Bible for their congregations. But we hope that as well as making a good case for striving toward that end as much as possible, we have supplied some helpful guidance for how you might start going about it and shown that, on almost every front, this approach will be beneficial for your congregations. We trust it will also be beneficial to you as you set a pattern that will deepen your understanding of God's word and, ultimately, your faithful discipleship and the joy it brings.

Some of Jesus's last words to the far-from-perfect apostle Peter were the directive to feed his lambs (John 21:15–19). Years later, Peter passed on this advice to the church leaders who read his first letter, exhorting them to "shepherd the flock of God" that was among them (1 Pet. 5:1–2). Peter then encouraged them by reminding them that if they were faithful to this charge, then "when the chief Shepherd appears, you will receive the unfading crown of glory" (v. 4). This is an unimaginably and incomparably wonderful prize, one that is perhaps bettered only by the good that we will be doing for our people and the glory that our ministry will be bringing to Jesus Christ himself. So we would also like to leave you with Jesus's charge as well as Paul's commitment: feed his lambs, and do not shrink from declaring to them the whole counsel of God.

# General Index

# Scripture Index